With Unfailing Dedication

Rural Teachers *in the* War Years

Elizabeth McLachlan

Elizabeth McLachlan

NEWEST PRESS

National Library of Canada Cataloguing in Publication Data
McLachlan, Elizabeth, 1957-
With unfailing dedication

ISBN 1-896300-48-0

1. Teachers--Alberta--History--20th century. 2. Teachers--Saskatchewan--History--20th century. 3. Education, Rural--Alberta--History--20th century. 4. Education, Rural--Saskatchewan--History--20th century. I. Title. LA2321.M339
2001   371.1'0092'2712   C2001-910791-9

Editor for the press: Satya Das
Copy editor: Carol Berger
Cover images: Top left: Students lined up to enter Abelein School, Albert, circa 1937. Courtesy of Elizabeth McLachlan. Top centre: Courtesy of the Provincial Archives of Alberta. Top right: Coaldale Consolidated School, Grade 8 class, 1939-1940. Courtesy of Elizabeth McLachlan. Bottom: Courtesy of the Provincial Archives of Alberta. Hazel Smith, one of the contributors. Courtesy of Hazel Smith.
Author photo: Dirk Brower Photography
Cover and interior design: Ruth Linka

Canadian Patrimoine
Heritage canadien

THE CANADA COUNCIL | LE CONSEIL DES ARTS
FOR THE ARTS | DU CANADA
SINCE 1957 | DEPUIS 1957

NeWest Press acknowledges the support of the Canada Council for the Arts and The Alberta Foundation for the Arts for our publishing program. We also acknowledge the financial support of the Government of Canada through the Book Publishing Industry Development Program (BPIDP) for our publishing activities.

NeWest Press
201-8540-109 Street
Edmonton, Alberta
T6G 1E6
t: (780) 432-9427
f: (780) 433-3179
www.newestpress.com

1 2 3 4 5 05 04 03 02 01

PRINTED AND BOUND IN CANADA

Dedicated once again to all those who entrusted their stories to me,
a virtual stranger, for the sake of posterity.

Acknowledgements

... Judy Hamill of CBC Radio for eliciting the idea

... Liz Grieve for encouraging it

... NeWest Board of Directors for accepting it

... Satya Das, my editor, for persistence, patience and calm helpfulness

... Ruth Linka and Erin Creasey of 'the Press' for assistance, efficience and unfailing friendliness

... Gladys Slemp and Marda Compton of Coronation Memorial Library for cheerfully going several extra miles for me

... Adele Pauls, Coaldale Public Library, for remaining unruffled at my strange research request. Her comment: "I like a bit of a challenge."

... Scott Robison, my nephew, for invaluable guidance in a last minute pinch

And of course Dale and Brandi, cherished beyond measure for *their* Unfailing Dedication.

Table of Contents

Introduction

. . . .

 "Extra! Extra! Read all about it! War declared! Hitler has invaded Poland!" My father was asleep in the 'cold bedroom' of great grandmother's house when he woke to the newsie's cry. The chill that swept through him had nothing to do with the 6:00 AM frostiness of a September 3rd morning in the southern Alberta prairie city of Lethbridge. For days he'd made the trek to the *Lethbridge Herald* building, checking the developments posted daily while Adolf Hitler "rattled the saber," and Britain and France crept closer to all-out war with Germany. Now it was here.

What would he do? He was set to begin a new teaching position in Coaldale in just two days. A dream job. After five years of multi-graded country schools he'd finally obtained a single grade in a town school. True, his uncle, the former principal, put in a good word for him, but that's what it took to get a job in 1939 when teachers were a dime a dozen. For ten long years rampant unemployment had cursed the country; a hallmark of the Great Depression. My father Murray, then a young bachelor of twenty-four, felt privileged to have worked at all.

Now patriotic urgings pricked his soul. He wanted to teach, but as part of the British Commonwealth, it was just a matter of time before Canada, too, would be at war. It would be right to enlist. His younger brother, nineteen and already in the Reserve Army, joined up immediately. Sergeant Norman Robison—Artillery, Anti-Aircraft—was one of the first to be shipped overseas.

Strangely, but like most who signed up, thoughts of fighting, destruction and death hardly entered Murray's mind. Instead it was "how I would ever be able to wear those dreadful wool flannel uniforms, my skin was so sensitive to wool!"

He needn't have feared. A pre-enlistment medical at the Lethbridge recruiting office sealed his fate. Bad eyes and bad feet. The army didn't want him. "I suppose I was relieved and yet disappointed at the same time," he recalls. "I know that Grandma was sure happy!"

So Murray began teaching grade eight at the Coaldale Consolidated School while war spread like cancer throughout Europe. Today we have the satisfaction of knowing who won, but sixty years ago there were no such assurances. With cunning intelligence Hitler carried out his plan to expand Germany into a world power. He'd already established a liaison with Benito Mussolini of Italy. Together the "axis" brought down country after country while Great Britain and France—the Allies—struggled just to gain the foothold necessary to launch an offensive.

German submarine attacks on merchant ships bound for Great Britain dealt a crippling blow to that country, while repeated smashings by air threatened to all but annihilate her. France, unable to continue her defence, watched German troops march into Paris in June of 1940.

When Japan joined the Axis, signing a military and economic pact with Germany and Italy, things looked grimmer and grimmer for the Allies. On the Canadian home front spirits dwindled. The question that played on everyone's minds was, "What if we lose?"

Then came "Pearl Harbor," the infamous Japanese air attack on the US navy in Hawaii and the Philippines. It was like a bee sting in the backside of a sleeping dog. The United States, which had thus far declared itself neutral, sprang into action. On 8 December 1941, the US and Great Britain declared war on Japan, and in turn Germany and Italy declared war on the United States.

A fresh surge of indignation and patriotic resolve spurred the country. Murray could no longer stand idle. "There was an air force recruiting office in Medicine Hat and I decided that if the army didn't want me perhaps the air force would take me into some capacity on ground crew. It just so happened that a new form of defence had been developed called "radar", a system of detecting enemy aircraft before it reached its target. It also just so happened that for radar one didn't have to have perfect eyesight or good feet to be engaged. I was in the forces at last."

Murray was ecstatic, but by enlisting he unwittingly became part of the problem that plagued the Canadian school system virtually from the war's beginning. Thousands of teachers flocked from their classrooms in a conscience-driven quest to do their bit for their country. War involvement wasn't restricted to men, or the armed forces. Many Canadian jobs were designated "essential to the war" and/or "war industries" and needed a great influx of employees to keep the war machine moving. Positions in these jobs were frozen. Those who held them were not allowed to leave while the conflict lasted, unless it was to join the conflict itself. Eventually teaching received an essential designation too, but not before thousands left the profession to enter war-related work.

Many joined the forces. Over 45,000 women, a good number of them teachers, volunteered for service in one of the three women's divisions: the Royal Canadian Air Force, the Women's Royal Canadian Naval Service, and the Canadian Women's Army

Corps. Dozens of students graduating from Normal School, the teacher training institution of the day, didn't wait to try out their new skills in the classroom. They marched straight into the military.

The ensuing crisis in Canadian schools, particularly country schools, cut swift and deep. Countless qualified teachers who'd literally begged for jobs during the depression simply vanished. Those left suddenly had the luxury of choice. Who could blame them for selecting town schools? Country schools left a lot to be desired in those days. Broken down buildings and sparse teaching supplies were the depression's legacy. The economic boom brought on by war didn't alleviate this. Not only were benefits slow to reach rural districts, but even when money was there, the necessary manpower and materials weren't. As many men as possible were needed for the war effort, and so were such things as building supplies and paper. (The planning and building of one battleship alone required 100 tons of paper.) Country schools continued to deteriorate.

Emilia (Vogel) Raab, who taught at the one-room Blarney School north of Compeer, Alberta in 1944, remembers that "the only supplies the school received were two boxes of white chalk, one box of coloured, one ball, one bat and of course the textbooks."

"I remember our dictionary which had many loose pages," she states. "If someone used it while the windows were open there were pages all over the classroom. If the ball's seams opened one of the boys took it home and fixed it . . . If the bat broke someone made one out of poplar wood."

Jeanette (Hahn) Miller, who taught forty students from grades one to ten in the Gouldtown School near Herbert, Saskatchewan in 1941, tells what happened when the fire in the wood stove wasn't started early enough on school mornings.

"The building was very cold as it was also poorly built, so we had physical training for an hour or so until we could remove our outdoor clothing. Since there was very little room with the forty-plus desks, P.T. consisted mostly of stretching and running on the spot."

Jeanette's experience was typical of many who taught in rural schools. She boarded with one of the families of the district. "It was a three-roomed home with a very large kitchen which served as dining room, living room and a bedroom at night as it had a cot which was made up for the two small sons."

There was no such thing as running water, electric lights, refrigeration or central heating. Coal oil or gasoline lanterns, wood stoves, root cellars and outhouses were the norm.

"Meals were very plain with little variety," she recalls, "and meat was seldom served. Fresh fruit wasn't around and I don't recall seeing canned fruit either. Occasionally we had eggs (produced on the farm) but I suspect they were mostly bartered to the store in exchange for food staples."

Jeanette walked to school with the boys.

"We soon found a shortcut (one and a quarter miles) climbing through fences and going through pastures. However, once the snow became deep the eleven-year-old took complete control of the reins and we travelled the three miles by horse and sled."

Even when Jeanette fell ill with a terrible cold she forced herself to continue going to school. "I felt it was my duty as there was no substitute teacher."

She was seventeen years old, 200 miles from home and extremely lonely. "There was no social life for me and weekends were long and boring."

With these conditions it's no wonder qualified schoolteachers were not anxious to teach in country schools. One after another, one-room rural schools were forced to shut their doors.

School boards scrambled to stem the tide of closures. During the depression, in order to free jobs for men, married women were not allowed to work. Now teachers who'd lost their status after marrying were pleaded with to return. Many had acquired the new roles of farm wife and mother and found the adjustment back to teaching far too difficult. Dorothy Murray was sick and pregnant with her first child when she was asked to teach at Sulpher Springs School in east-central Alberta. She lasted one month—most of it in the outhouse. But she wasn't let off the hook. After having her baby she was approached again. Marquis, her husband's home school near their farm, would close if she didn't take it over. She was a young wife, anxious to make a good impression in her new community. She felt she had no choice but to do it.

Another former teacher, Lillian Coulson, was living in Edmonton when war broke out. "My husband joined the air force. I wondered how my young son and I would survive on seventy-seven dollars a month, paid by the government to service men's dependents. The home school where I had taught for several years (Orangeville, near Sangudo, Alberta) had no teacher. I received an sos to teach there again. I accepted the offer because I could live with my widowed mother and walk the mile to school."

Older, retired teachers were appealed to as well. Here British Prime Minister Sir Winston Churchill had an unexpected influence. Well into his sixties when in 1940 he took on the Prime Ministership and the war, he set a shining example for every senior to do his or her part. Valleyview, Alberta resident, Mary Werklund recalls that her mother, Bessie Caldwell, who retired from teaching in 1934, returned to the profession in 1941. Several years later and still in the classroom, "she would catnap and the children would whisper and tip-toe around so as not to waken her." But Bessie was determined. "If Winston Churchill can do it," she declared, "I can do my best too!"

Retired teachers and recalled housewives weren't enough, however, and the shortage grew worse. A war emergency call went out across the provinces summoning anyone with even a modicum of interest in teaching to respond to the crisis.

Ruby (Plomp) Anderson, who attended grade twelve at La-Riviere, Manitoba in 1943, had "never considered becoming a teacher."

"About Easter-time," she recalls, "our principal received a letter from the Department of Education asking that he encourage some of his graduating class to consider applying for admission to a six-week Special Course for Prospective Permit Teachers. It would be held in July and August in Winnipeg. No fee would be charged . . . Books required would cost about ten dollars. Our signatures on the application forms would be taken as evidence that we agreed to attend Normal School on the expiration of the permit [one year]. Ten dollars per month would be deducted from our salaries and applied to Normal School fees. On completion of the summer course we would be placed in schools by the Department. We would not be allowed to answer advertisements for teachers or apply for schools on our own behalf. However, our school inspector told us we would be able to give a choice as to where we wished to go."

This temporary permit program lasted until well after the war. Lucille (Wood) Thompson remembers that "there was still a call for permit teachers" in 1946. She was sixteen years old when she made her way to #3 Wireless Army Station in Winnipeg. "There were still soldiers on guard duty at the gate," she recalls, "but the rest was now 'Normal' School where we would spend six weeks on a crash course to be able to go out into one-room rural schools. We slept in barracks: iron bunk beds, army-issue bedding, common bathroom, ate in the mess hall. Classes were held in a large building, which was there before it was an army base. The teachers crammed as much as possible into those six weeks, not so much subject matter, but how to present the subject as [we] would be expected to teach everything from Art to Math to Physical Activity."

Lucille was assigned the Marland School west of Cardale. She credits her survival to the excellent teachers she'd had as a child. "I drew on my remembrance of them to organize and teach."

She had little else.

"I can remember the hectograph," she says, "and science equipment, which consisted of one test tube, one beaker and a bunsen burner. We did the best we could and received the princely sum of $750 for ten months work—and [we] paid room and board—and as a teacher you had to be well dressed."

The six-week training program still didn't generate enough personnel, and in some cases it was waived. Lenore (Warkentine) Loewen, Caroline (Parobeck) Antoniw and Joyce (Kay) Rushton, whose stories appear in this book, took over rural one-room schools with virtually no training. Neil Bergen of Manitoba was assigned a school with forty-three students in eight grades the day he graduated from grade twelve. "It was a hell of a way to learn to teach" is his only comment.

Alberta tried to avoid this potential for disaster by converting its teacherless schools to correspondence centres. Shirley (Magee) McKibbin was "fresh out of grade eleven" in 1944. "The Department of Education had conceived a plan of allowing unlicensed teenagers to take the schools and supervise correspondence lessons," she states. "We were given a crash course in keeping a register, setting up a timetable and looking after fires at school and at home. We spent two or three days observing in schools that had regular teachers. It was a real eye-opener for those of us who were familiar with only one grade in a room."

Officially the supervisor's duties were to take attendance, distribute the lessons, and send them back for grading to the Correspondence School Branch in Edmonton. Unofficially they did much more.

In the meantime Normal Schools worked hard to get would-be teachers into schools faster. Age and course requirements were relaxed. In Saskatchewan in 1942 Normal Schools accepted students who did not have grade twelve. In addition, they established a system whereby Normalites were churned out into country schools every twelve weeks on a rotating basis (four times a year). Between 1942 and 1945, 3,880 teachers were placed in this manner. It mattered little how much training a neophyte had—only that he or she had some training at all.

Freda (Daymon) Longman was a student at the Regina Normal School only three months before she was asked to go out and teach.

"At age eighteen I found myself in charge of thiry-one pupils [at Happy Centre School near Willowbrook], grades one to ten as well as one mentally handicapped child."

During the war a severe shortage of farm labour kept older children home to help during harvest and other busy times of the year. School boards tended to turn a blind eye to this with the result that many students fell behind in their grades. The age gap between novice teacher and pupil, never very wide, narrowed even more. Freda had one student older than she was and another the same age. She counts herself lucky that she had no discipline problems. "Some other young teachers had real horror stories to tell."

Freda's youth was accentuated one day as she dismissed the school for lunch.

"One of the pupils asked if they were to go home then as it was Election Day and they always had the afternoon off so the teacher could go to vote. I had to explain that I wasn't old enough to vote! You had to be twenty-one at that time. If you can imagine, I was old enough to teach school and many boys were fighting for their country but we weren't old enough to vote!"

Age didn't exempt Freda from responsibility. As the only 'adult' authority on the premises she had no choice but to cope with every situation that arose. One student sustained a badly broken knee on the ball diamond, another suffered an epileptic seizure, and another fell hard and put her tooth through her lip. Fortunately Freda was close enough to catch the girl who fainted from the stage to the floor during a Christmas concert practice.

"We had no phone in the school," she explains. "The first aid kit patched up the usual cuts and scrapes but the more serious cases were handled by asking two older pupils to hitch up a pony and cart and take the patient to his home, usually two, three or more miles from the school."

Freda coped with the effects of vandalism as well. With her first precious paycheque she bought a wristwatch because "every time they put a clock in the school it was stolen."

"Until I got my watch," she says, "I had to carry an alarm clock to school each day, loaned by my landlady!"

Freda obviously made a good impression on the district. They threw her a surprise party and presented her with a pen and pencil set the last day of school.

"I had just finished correcting exams and making out all the report cards when they came in. To my horror, I burst into tears. Looking back now, I'm sure it was because of a very stressful year and a half for an eighteen-year-old on my first job."

Freda taught for sixteen months after just three months of Normal School. By contrast, in Alberta Normal students were sent into rural schools for eight- to twelve-week teaching stints, after which they returned to Normal and a fresh batch of Normalites were sent out to replace them. In *Classroom Classics Too*, edited by Anne Lindgren, Doris Erickson of Ponoka relates: "We were paid one dollar a day and room and board, transportation and a refund of one third of our $100 tuition. We were not required to catch up classes we had missed." By 1943 Alberta high school graduates were permitted to take over rural schools after twelve weeks of training, and grade eleven students with a minimum B standing in Social Studies and English could in seven months achieve both their high school diploma and a special "war emergency interim teachers certificate."

It's incredible to think of these young people stepping more or less cold into jobs normally reserved for the professionally trained. It's even more incredible to consider that on top of their extreme youth and lack of preparation they were forced to contend with the same isolation, homesickness, and inadequate living and working conditions that had plagued trained teachers for years.

Yet for many it was perceived as the chance to do something for their country. Perhaps they were too young to join the armed forces, but this they could do. They shouldered the task with the same spirit of determination and fortitude as those who had left for the front lines.

In years since, many have criticized this period in history as one in which the education of Canadian schoolchildren suffered dreadfully at the hands of under-aged, under-qualified personnel. That may be so. But were it not for these brave teens agreeing to undertake unbelievable challenges and hardships, the education of the country's children would have been far further compromised. Regardless of the outcome, they stepped forward in their country's time of need. Children teaching children. No one can question their courage.

Shirley

Shirley Magee (now McKibbin) had never tended a fire. She'd never been to a one-room school, never looked after a whole roomful of juveniles, and in her short seventeen years certainly never lived alone. Yet at the height of the war in 1944 she was "longing to do something worthwhile." Her application for the women's division of the RCAF had been painstakingly filled out but never sent. It frustrated her to no end that she was too young to join up.

Shirley attended the town school in Stettler, Alberta. Her family was good friends with the division superintendent's family. Neighbours, in fact. When he asked Shirley if she would supervise in the rural Stewartwyn School nearby, her eyes lit up. Here was her chance to make a difference! Even though it meant delaying her own grade twelve education she jumped at the opportunity.

A brief training session hardly prepared Shirley for the task at hand, but it did teach her some basic survival skills. One was how to light a fire in a stove and keep it burning properly so that neither she nor the children froze to death or died of toxic fumes.

Good knowledge to have because Stewartwyn School sat alone on a bleak, windswept corner. A tiny one-room teacherage went with it, but nobody was in favour of a young girl living alone there. It was easy to pick up the shed-like building and put it on skids to move it to the nearest farm. Shirley's first yard was a pasture, but at least there were people just through the trees and across the lane.

Shirley's mother accompanied her to the new home. One look at the mean dwelling and she rolled up her sleeves. With a determined glint in her eye she fell to the task of making it habitable. The entire place was scrubbed to a shine, the two windows dressed with bright fabric and towels and bedding brought in. Shirley remembers the frying pan requiring her mother's special treatment. Grimy with layers of old grease, it was thrust into the hot stove and left to 'burn off'. "When it was scoured and seasoned it was as good as new," she proudly recalls.

All that was needed next was a washstand and cupboard. Wooden orange crates supplied by the Stettler grocer filled the bill nicely.

It was living, if not at its finest.

"I found that I could sit at the table and reach anything on the bed or the stove," says Shirley. "I had running water only if I moved fast enough when I carried it from the well."

Outhouses were new to a girl who'd always lived in town. She shared with the farm family and remembers "a long chilly walk to the 'wee' house."

That wasn't all that was chilly. As winter drew in the teacherage became unbearably cold. She couldn't understand why until she mentioned it to her father when she went home for Christmas. After the holidays he took her back and was appalled to discover the wooden structure sitting several inches off the ground, allowing the wind a merry course beneath it. Bales and packed snow soon took care of that.

But Shirley, just a schoolgirl herself, was unaccustomed to living on her own. The nights were lonely, with no way of getting around to visit farm neighbours. The only consolation was her radio. Powered by a wet battery, it provided many hours of comfort, especially on Saturdays when the Metropolitan Opera Company delighted listeners with glorious music.

By spring, Shirley decided she'd had enough of fending for herself. "A Scottish couple took pity on me and asked if I'd like to stay with them. It was wonderful; good meals, a snug bed and good company."

Problems with the teacherage aside, Shirley had little apprehension about supervising in a one-room school. "The first few weeks were marvelous," she recalls, "with only the little ones present. The older children were on harvest leave, doing men's work on the farms."

Shirley was thoroughly enjoying her time with the youngsters when one day late in the fall two grade nine boys walked in. One of them towered over her! As Shirley scrambled to gather her wits she endeavoured to appear calm. But her panic betrayed her.

"Talk about nerves! I missed part of the Lord's Prayer that morning, after having repeated it since I was a little girl! Needless to say, I said it over and over that night."

Unlike many young girls who supervised, Shirley needn't have worried about the presence of the big boys. They turned out to be helpful beyond measure.

"Through the long winter they made certain that the little ones were buttoned and booted with toques and mittens on properly before they let them out into the cold."

Instead, Shirley encountered adversity in a far less likely area. Other teachers! At first they were kind when supervisors came to observe in their classrooms. Even though the supervisors were untrained, teachers recognized the vital role they played in keeping rural schools open. Then word got out about what the supervisors were paid. Only slightly less than the teachers! Shirley made seventy dollars a month while many fully qualified, experienced teachers still made far less than $100. At that time an adequate wage for living, according to the Alberta Teachers Association, was a minimum $120 a month (based on a ten-month year).

There was an uproar. The previously cooperative attitude of the teachers cooled perceptibly. Soon the derisive term "sitters" began to circulate, and supervisors were made subtly unwelcome at teachers' meetings. The ATA was not pleased either. In addition to their schoolwork, teachers were encouraged to help on farms during the holidays. This was prompted by the serious labour shortage combined with hiking demands for farm produce to help feed the troops and the people of Great Britain. The editor of the May 1944 issue of *The ATA Magazine* wondered at the paradox of teachers being recruited for farm work while farm children were recruited to "supervise" in schools.

All this, according to Shirley, made teachers meetings "a bit difficult."

Shirley may have been considered a mere "sitter," but the expectations placed upon her by district parents, Stettler School Division trustees and indeed the Department of National Defence were very much adult. That year it was discovered that the Japanese were attempting to sabotage Canadian soil by floating "hot air balloon bombs" across the Pacific and over Western Canada. On impact of touchdown, a chemical reaction triggered in the balloon's mechanism causing the paper balloon to burst into flames. The Japanese hoped the resulting fires would destroy acres and acres of forests and farmland, resources vital to the war effort. A special strategy was needed to arrest the attacks while avoiding panic among the public. Rural schoolteachers and supervisors were uniquely situated to help. They were perceived as especially responsible, and also had access to knowledge about everything that went on in their districts. Shirley and others were entrusted with a top-secret mission.

"Sometime in the fall the superintendent arrived with an official looking letter from the Department of Defence. I was allowed to read it but couldn't keep it and I was to say nothing about its contents."

It wasn't until years later that the subject of those letters came out. The teachers and supervisors were to keep eyes and ears open, reporting to the RCMP any unusual incidents that might be related to the balloon bombs. The news blackout not only prevented public panic over an impending Japanese invasion, but it effectively convinced the Japanese that their plan wasn't working. They ultimately terminated the campaign.

Not all of Shirley's adult responsibilities came off so well. As schoolhouses were often the only public building in the district they also served as meeting hall, dance hall, church, and all-round community centre. Who better to play the role of social convener than the schoolteacher? When teachers left to join the war effort, for some reason districts assumed that their teenage replacements would naturally take over every facet of the job. This included organizing social events for the entire district.

Supervisors were left in a no-win situation. They were expected to behave like adults yet obey like children. Even if they didn't feel capable of pulling off a community function they didn't dare say no when asked to do it.

Shirley's turn came when the district began to weary of the long winter. At first, she recalls, all went well:

"The neighbours decided that we should have a dance at the

school. The men provided the transportation, the ladies lunch, and a local band provided music."

One of the sad realities of war, however, is that it throws natural order into chaos. When men and women are forced to live apart sexual tension flares and infidelity is rampant. A dance, however innocent, was fertile ground for trouble. Shirley likens what she witnessed at the Stewartwyn dance to Eugene Field's nursery poem about the Gingham Dog and the Calico Cat who, *"employing every tooth and claw in the awfullest way you ever saw,"* tore each other apart.

"One woman cosied up to the husband of another and the fight was on. They disgraced themselves by scratching and screeching and pulling hair. Monday morning, before school, I swept up handfuls of dark hair. There must have been a couple of sore heads in the district. That was our last attempt at entertainment."

Spring brought reprieve, made sweeter by the second hand bike Shirley's father found for her.

"It wasn't pretty, but I was fortunate to get one in wartime."

Metal and rubber were rationed materials. They were highly in demand for war equipment. Rubber in particular became virtually inaccessible after the Japanese invaded the Dutch East Indies, whose rubber plants supplied the world. The manufacture of consumer products containing these materials all but ceased as long as the war raged.

The precious bicycle opened the world to Shirley. She rode great distances to acquaint herself with rural neighbours she'd never met. Best of all, on mild weekends she biked home to Stettler on Friday and back again Sunday. Occasionally a friend from Stettler loaded her bike into his car and drove her back to school Monday morning, so she enjoyed the added pleasure of staying home Sunday night as well.

Before she knew it June arrived and the school year was over. Her grade nine boys wrote their departmental exams and the whole school took part in a year-end picnic. Shirley would not return to Stewartwyn. It was time to go back to Stettler and finish her own education.

Even though she fondly recalls her year as one she'll "never forget or regret," Shirley paid a price for her contribution to the war effort.

"September brought the most difficult year of my life," she relates. "I was back in school taking directions instead of giving them. My friends had graduated and were off doing their things. My sister and her friends were now in the same classes."

Nevertheless, Shirley had been smitten by the 'teaching bug'. She graduated and went on to the University of Alberta, where a special one-year certificate program put her back into the classroom—this time as a bona fide teacher.

"The Alberta government paid our tuition but we had to agree to teach for three years in Alberta or pay it back."

Shirley furthered her training by attending summer school for several years. She taught until 1967 when, she states with satisfaction, "I retired after having answered school bells since I was five years old!"

Carrie

· ·

· · · · · · · · · · · · · · · ·

Carrie Gadsden (now Anderson) was one of the first Six-Week Wonders—young people given accreditation as teachers after only six weeks of training. The label was often applied with the same derision as "sitters." A perspective of sixty years, however, has made it clear that these individuals were indeed wonders.

"I had my eighteenth birthday the middle of October and was out teaching the first of November," states Carrie. "We were given the name of the school we were to go to, the name and address of our landlady-to-be and a return railway ticket to our destination."

What a way to begin thiry-five years of teaching!

In 1943, mixed trains (long freight trains with a passenger coach attached) were still a common form of travel. Carrie boarded the midnight mixed from Calgary and sixteen weary hours later found herself in another world. Completely alone, family and friends left far behind, she stood on the Glenevis station platform, bewildered by the confusion of foreign words around her. Just as panic threatened to overtake her a man approached and, to her enormous relief, asked, in English, if she was the new schoolteacher for Greenhill School. The title was as foreign to Carrie as the language she'd just heard, but she was quick to say yes! Trunks and "teacher" safely bundled onto horse and wagon, she set off into the unknown once more.

It truly was unknown. Carrie had graduated from Crescent Heights High School in the city of Calgary. She'd never experienced more than one grade to a room and readily admits she "had no idea how a country school operated." But she had listened well during her six weeks at Calgary Normal School. She knew how to draw up a timetable and prepare lesson plans. She was armed and ready with both the morning she faced twenty students for the first time.

What a shock to discover that neither worked!

"One period I was supposed to be teaching three grades at once. The next period everyone was doing seatwork and I was idle. It didn't take me long to figure out that this would never do so I soon had a workable timetable."

It's a good thing Carrie was quick to catch on, for she was left on her own for weeks. By the time the inspector put in an appearance it was almost Christmas and Carrie had sorted out all her problems on her own.

"At the end of the afternoon he told me he owed me an apology. He said all the other students were sent for a day to observe in a country school. It was so long since this school had a teacher he forgot I was there."

Adjusting to a country school required more than just figuring out timetables. Imagine Carrie's dismay the first time she set eyes on the log construction that was her school. There were numerous gaps between the ancient timbers and one entire corner was propped up by a large rock.

"The wind whipped under the building in this corner so it was very cold in winter," she shudders. "I had to wear my ski pants and snowboots all day to keep warm. The ink froze overnight and didn't thaw until afternoon so most of the written work had to be done in pencil."

The inside of the school was drab and poor. Nothing but brown paper lined the walls. Of course the rain soaked through in the spring. When the sodden paper could hold no more, water seeped out over the floor.

"Having grown up in the city I assumed everyone would come to school neatly dressed, including shoes," remembers Carrie. "When some of the children arrived in bare feet I told them this wasn't acceptable and they must wear shoes in the classroom. The next day along they came in bare feet carrying their shoes. When I found out later how poor some of these families were I was a little embarrassed. What if they hadn't owned a pair of shoes? One girl in grade eight wore her brother's hand-me-down overalls. Her only dress was made from flour sacks."

The flour sack dress was fit for a princess the day the whole school attended the Spring Festival in the nearby hamlet of Cherhill. Carrie was astonished to discover that the children had never been. Determined to provide them with the unique and exciting experience she enlisted the help of one of her students' older brothers. He agreed to take them all to Cherhill in the back of his truck. Everything would've gone smoothly if it hadn't rained heavily the night before, transforming dirt roads into rivers of mud. The truck ground to a halt in the muck. By the time they all pitched in to dislodge it they were late for the festival. The girl in the flour sack dress missed competing in her category. The kindly adjudicator, however, consented to hear her recitation when all the others had finished. She gave a dazzling presentation and was awarded first place in her class. The entire school stayed for the special evening performance of the winners. It was the thrill of the year for Carrie and the students, and the thrill of a lifetime for the girl in the flour sack dress.

Even though school began eight weeks late that year, Carrie needed only two extra weeks at the end of June to get the students through their work. Every one of them passed their exams and advanced to the next grade. Not bad for a six-week wonder!

Three summer school sessions later at the University of Alberta and Carrie herself advanced to being a full-fledged, fully qualified teacher. She never looked back.

Joyce

Sometime in the early 1970s Joyce Rushton took a phone call at home. It was one of the teachers of the Virden Manitoba school in which she taught.

"Are you coming to the meeting tonight to demand higher wages?" he wanted to know.

"Don't be ridiculous," she answered. "I'd teach for nothing if I had to."

Such was the dedication of the girl who thirty years earlier walked into a rural Manitoba school, regarded a roomful of young faces gazing expectantly up at her and thought, "What am I doing here?"

What indeed? Her father lived in Alberta, she had just graduated from Naicam High School in Saskatchewan, and she had only been in Winnipeg for the summer, visiting her sisters Madge and Rene before returning to Saskatchewan to attend Normal School in Regina.

It was a wonderful summer. Full of new friends, shopping, movies and big city sights. She'd even had a job as a governess to make money for new clothes. As she was packing to leave at the end of August, Madge buttonholed her.

"Why go back to Saskatchewan?" she argued. "It's not fair that our sister there gets to keep you. It's time you were with us.

Why not teach in Manitoba?"

Madge then called in the reinforcements. She phoned the Registrar's office of the Manitoba Department of Education and told them she had a sister packing her bags that very moment for the Regina Normal School. What were they prepared to do about it?

"If there's a real live person that can teach walking around get her up here!" was the Registrar's response. In 1943 the situation in Manitoba was so desperate that when Madge and Joyce arrived at the Legislative Building the Registrar placed a sheaf of papers before Joyce and said, "Those are 200 Manitoba schools that need you!"

Joyce had her pick. She naturally chose the school closest to Winnipeg so she could visit her sisters during holidays. The Registrar signed her up for South Head School, then dropped his bombshell. She must commit to attending Normal School the following year in Manitoba, not Saskatchewan. Joyce enthusiastically agreed.

"Madge took me and my luggage to the train station," she says, "and I set off as Miss Kay to my first school."

She was just two weeks shy of her eighteenth birthday and she had received no preparation whatsoever. Excitement soon transformed to butterflies.

"I stood in front of about twenty students from grade two to eight and I didn't know what I was doing there. I thought, 'What a ridiculous thing; me standing here thinking I knew anything.'"

What's more, Joyce had been warned about a "bad boy" who'd deliberately made things so miserable for the previous teacher, she'd packed up and left.

"There was 'Albert' [not his real name], in the front row, sizing me up."

He was a head taller than Joyce and she swallowed hard as she tried to decide quickly how to deal with him.

"Albert," she finally said to the boy as he delivered her a challenging stare, "I'd like to see you at recess, just for a little talk."

To help the children get used to her Joyce spent the morning reading to them, but running through her mind the whole time was the upcoming meeting with Albert. When recess came the children ran out to play. Albert, hostility tinged with curiosity, slouched up to her desk.

"I'm so very busy," Joyce began, "and I was just wondering, since you're the oldest in the school, if you'd be my playground supervisor."

Albert's eyes widened in disbelief. Joyce went on.

"With no windows on the playground side of the school I can't see what the children are doing. If you see anybody pushing anyone around and you can't stop it yourself, come in and tell me and I'll stop it."

By now the boy's shoulders had pulled back and his chest was out. He agreed to help Miss Kay. When the children returned she addressed the entire school.

"I hope you realize that Albert is keeping an eye out for your behaviour and seeing that you follow the softball rules and everything—because he answers to me."

The surprised children looked from Joyce to Albert. They had all expected him to be expelled at any time. Now his authority over them was second only to the teacher's.

"From that day on," says Joyce, "he came to be my staunchest ally. He would settle arguments, ump and score ball games, and tell me if a problem was too big for him. He was a big help. I had no trouble all year."

Joyce's first triumph bolstered her. Never one to see obstacles as anything but a challenge, she applied herself to the task of learning how to teach. She studied and re-studied the rules in the back of the school register and taught herself how to prepare lesson plans and keep the children happily productive. Nevertheless, she was painfully aware of her lack of training and because of it was certain she'd be fired.

The last Friday of the month arrived and so did the school board secretary.

"This is it," thought Joyce, but instead he produced her first paycheque. Seventy dollars minus ten dollars for next year's Normal School.

"I couldn't believe it," she recalls. "I thought: 'I've fooled them for a month. Maybe I can fool them for another!'"

But month after month the cheques kept coming. Joyce continued to gain favour with the children and their parents. Her confidence grew and the terror of the first days gradually disappeared. One more hurdle, however, loomed before her. The intimidating Mrs. Brooks!

"She was my first inspector," explains Joyce. "When I heard she was to inspect me and my classroom I was sure my career was finished before it began."

Joyce makes an understatement when she says, "The students came through for me and made me look okay, so I got a good report." In fact the Registrar, Mr. Bennett, later told her that he'd never received a better report from an inspector.

Joyce enjoyed happy circumstances at her boarding place too. Mr. and Mrs. Chambers welcomed her with open arms. They were a wonderful couple. Mrs. Chambers, especially, was a beautiful cook. Compared to other rural teachers who often paid twice as much, Joyce's living arrangements were a steal.

"I boarded for fifty cents a day, and when I was in Winnipeg for Christmas and Easter Mrs. Chambers wouldn't take the fifty cents because I hadn't eaten there."

By the end of the year Joyce had wound herself round everyone's hearts. They begged her to stay. She knew she couldn't because her permit was only for one year, conditional upon attending Normal School the next. As those around her became more insistent she began to worry. She took the unprecedented step of phoning Mr. Bennett, asking him to refuse when the school board requested her return.

"You see," she explains, "I wanted training and I wanted to go on to a bigger school."

Normal School was a breeze. "I really didn't learn a great deal because I had [already] struggled through most of what they were trying to teach us. Just the same I went through the whole ten months."

At the end of the year Joyce was exempted from writing her final exams.

September 1945 she was assigned a junior high position in Waskada, Manitoba. It included the vice-principalship and a most attractive salary of $1,250 a year. Joyce was told that the people of Waskada were really special. Time proved it true, but not before several of the bigger boys hatched their plan for Miss Kay's first day.

"'Roy', Ernie, Bob and Harry stood by my desk the first recess and announced, 'We were the ones who gave the last teacher a nervous breakdown.' I lay down my pen, looked at them with steely eyes and informed them that if anyone was to have a nervous breakdown it would be them."

Ernie, Bob and Harry quickly backed off, but "Roy" was a tough nut to crack. Joyce recognized shades of "Albert" and soon came up with a plan.

"'Roy' was very good in math, so when a tough question came up I would ask him to put his solution on the board. I instructed the rest of the grade eights to copy it down.'Roy' realized he had value and slowly became a good student."

Joyce had an agreeable year in Waskada, but there were complications of a personal nature. Pretty young schoolteachers always sparked a great deal of attention from single men of the district.

"One of the fellows was getting a little interested so I called my dad and told him I was coming home to Alberta to look after him. He said, 'Am I sick again?' And I said, 'Yes, you're deathly ill.'"

So Joyce left for Alberta. By this time she was thoroughly in love with teaching and soon found a job at the newly built Dewberry School. Again she taught junior high and took on the role of vice-principal, but this time she signed a contract for a whopping $4,000 a year.

"It was tremendous money in the forties," she recalls. "Then of course the fellow that got interested in me wanted to visit Alberta. He came—and proposed to me—and after that I married him. So that's as far as I got."

But that's not as far as she got. Joyce and Glen Rushton returned to Waskada and farmed for many years. When her children were twelve and nine she went back to her great love and taught for a total of twenty-six years.

Her legacy continues.

"I have four nieces who followed in my tracks. Their mother says they all went in for teaching because of Aunt Joyce."

Magdalene

· ·
· · · · · · · · · · · · · · · · ·

 A young girl on a farm near Ponoka went out to feed the cows one evening in the mid 1930s. She gazed at the moon shimmering above the central Alberta prairie and made a vow: "Someday I'm going to see that over Big Ben."

It was a dream destined for fulfilment, for Magdalene Ungstad was an adventuress. She wasted no time getting on with her ambitions. Before she was twenty the first of life's many excitements was at hand.

In 1945 superintendents from across the province visited Magdalene's class at the Edmonton Normal School. They came with lists of schools that needed teachers and urged the Normalites to make their selection. Magdalene's choice was as far from familiar territory as she could get—the north. That's where adventure lay! She chose the Royal Winner School, eight miles west of Wanham in the Peace River region of Alberta. Magdalene and three like-minded friends packed their bags and set out.

Gerry left the train at Falher to teach in a French Catholic school. Audrey disembarked in Spirit River where her brother Dick was a school principal. They were the lucky ones. Doris, a girl who'd never been out of the city, found adventure whether she wanted it or not. In an isolated country school she had forty-seven children, including seventeen in grade one who couldn't speak English. There are only six hours of daylight in the northern winter. On her three-mile walk in darkness to and from school each day she carried two lanterns to keep the dogs that followed her at bay. She later found out they were wolves.

Magdalene encountered wolves of a different kind, but more of that later. Her school was south of the Burnt River; the students crossed the river to attend school from the north. The teacherage wasn't ready so when Magdalene first arrived she stayed with the neighbours nearest the school. They were members of a strict religious sect. Without Magdalene's knowledge they conceived what they considered a brilliant plan. Marry the teacher to a man from their church! With her contact with all the families of the district and his knowledge of the Bible they could take the Peace by storm, converting the entire region. Wedding arrangements began.

Magdalene had no idea. She set about establishing herself at the school and helping her students re-adjust after several years of correspondence lessons. She loved them dearly, and they were so grateful to finally have a teacher that they worked hard. One pupil caught up on four years of math in six months.

But before even two weeks had passed Magdalene began getting strange signals. At her boarding place she shared a bed with another of her pupils, a common practice in those days as few struggling farm families had extra room for the teacher. Magdalene's bedmate, a little girl, kept bubbling over about an upcoming wedding.

"There's going to be a wedding next Saturday," she beamed. "George, [not his real name], is getting married!"

Magdalene had met George, sitting across from her as a guest at the dinner table. She thought to herself, "I wouldn't marry that man if he was the last one on a desert island!"

Little did she realize that she was indeed the man's intended. The bride-to-be was blushing all right—blushing with anger as reality dawned. She put a swift halt to the plot, displeasing her benefactors mightily. Magdalene wasn't fazed, but it did put her in an awkward situation at her boarding house. When she received a telegram saying that her mother was dying and a train ticket home to Ponoka awaited her at the Wanham station, she left that boarding place for good.

The train "going out" (a phrase still used by people leaving the north for more southerly regions) ran from 4:00 PM until 8:30 AM. To pass the time Magdalene played cards with a couple she met on the coach. At five minutes past midnight a strange sensation enveloped her. She raised her head and solemnly stated, "My mother just died."

After the funeral Magdalene called the school board and told them she wouldn't return to the little school atop the Burnt River valley unless the teacherage was ready for occupancy. She took it a step further and also demanded isolation pay. She got it. Her wage of sixty-eight dollars a month fell far short of the ninety dollars her twin sister made wrapping bread in a bakery.

Magdalene took her younger sister back to live with her in the teacherage. Twelve-year-old Dede had a special gift, an ear for music. Whistle a tune and she could play it. She brought along her accordion and when the conductor saw it he allowed her to bring it aboard the train without checking it into the baggage compartment. He even asked her to play. The train was full of servicemen who were soon attracted by the music. Before long a hearty sing-along was underway. "Roll Out the Barrel," "The White Cliffs of Dover," "There'll Always Be an England," and other popular wartime ballads cheered them. The men were so impressed by Dede's playing that they tossed quarters to her, resulting in a small windfall for the young girl.

As evening wore on Dede showed signs of exhaustion and Magdalene put a halt to the singing. The servicemen were gallant. They treated the girls to dinner and one officer ordered a lower berth cleared for them. Dede and Magdalene had expected to sit up in the train throughout the night. Now they could stretch out and get some sleep after the trying days they'd just been through. The officer gave his personal word that no one would bother them.

There was a stop in Spirit River before changing trains for Wanham, so the girls picked up groceries. At the Wanham station the school board secretary met them and drove them out to the newly refurbished teacherage. He carried in their groceries, lit the fire and left. When Magdalene and Dede had a chance to look around they were utterly dismayed. One small bedroom contained a bed, a space-heater and a closet. Fortunately, Magdalene's father had shipped them some bedding. The kitchen/dining/living room had a table, one chair, a stove (the girls had to cut and split their own wood), water pail, hand basin, one saucepan, one beat up, loose-handled frying pan that was so warped they had to dint it to make it sit flush with the stove—and no dishes. They dragged in an old nail keg for a second chair and like Shirley in Stewartwyn put together two double orange crates to use as a washstand. For the privilege of living in these surroundings Magdalene paid eight dollars a month.

The first night they were hungry so thought they'd save time by opening a tin of beans rather than cooking the meat and potatoes they'd brought. They might as well have cooked. There was no can opener so they took after the tin with a gooseneck crowbar. It took some effort but they finally got into it. They set the mangled can into the hot coals of the stove to heat. No spoons. Magdalene used her imagination. She crawled into the dugout beneath the teacherage and tore a broad splinter from a beam. With this they ate their beans.

Getting water also required innovation. A well was dug several feet from a swamp with the idea that filtration from the swamp to the well would have a cleansing effect. It wasn't so. Even Raleigh's drink mixture couldn't mask the taste of 'swamp'. To avoid the taint the girls melted snow or collected dusty tasting rainwater as it ran off the roof.

When food supplies dwindled Magdalene and Dede estimated what time the train passed nearest the teacherage, then walked to the tracks and flagged it down with a red kerchief. The first time they did this the train squealed to a halt and an alarmed engineer asked, "What's wrong?"

Magdalene explained that they wanted to board. When she was reminded that the regular stop was another three miles up the track she sweetly replied, "If you want, we won't get on now. We'll walk ahead of the train to the stop and you can pick us up there."

The ladies were allowed on. From then on, whenever they needed groceries they flagged the train down in this manner. It pulled slowly by until the first coach drew up to them. Then the door opened and they were invited to step aboard. The train carried them to Rycroft where they bought groceries, and dropped the girls off again in the same spot going home.

Because single rural teachers were always very popular with the bachelors of the district, Magdalene of course had potential suitors. She also had no intention of getting married. She wanted to see the world! In fairness to both herself and the boys however, she allowed herself one compromise. If she met a boy she liked she'd date him, but after six weeks if she wasn't interested she'd break it off. That was her rule. It held her in good stead with the "good guys" of the district. But there were others ...

Many Friday night dances were held in Prestville and other nearby halls. People travelled from miles around to attend. It was common knowledge that two young ladies lived alone in the isolated teacherage. More than once inebriated men showed up to 'visit' after the dance. These occurrences were annoying.

One night a car full of drunken men stopped on the road outside the teacherage. Magdalene prayed they'd go away, but after a minute they drove through the gate. She grabbed the butcher knife. Her first thought was to jam the door shut with it, but when that didn't work she stood in the window brandishing the knife.

"I was determined and cool," she remembers. "All I could think of was, 'I'm going to protect my sister.'"

One sight of the nasty blade gleaming in her hand and the men quickly reconsidered. The car scooted away.

Magdalene was fed up. She reported all the episodes to the RCMP, who promptly passed word that anyone stopping uninvited and unwanted at the teacherage would be charged. For her part, Magdalene made little effort to dispel the rumour that the teacher kept a butcher knife and was not afraid to use it! She never had problems again.

By June she was ready to move on. Dede returned to Ponoka; Magdalene, Doris and Audrey reunited to teach in the recently enlarged South Slope School in Wanham. The first year they shared the new teacherage, but when Audrey left and a new principal with a family arrived, Magdalene and Doris gave up the teacherage and moved into the old one-room school, which had been converted into living quarters.

It was draughty and cold. Heat came from an old oil drum set on its side and given legs, a door, and a table-like top. Despite gobbling enormous amounts of wood it was able neither to keep ice from forming in the water pail nor the curlered heads of the girls from freezing to their pillows.

They slept on a Winnipeg couch close to the stove in the living room. When the back of the couch was let down to form a bed a deep crease marked the thin mattress. Doris and Magdalene replaced this mattress with the one from the bed in the bedroom (which was far too cold to sleep in), then for warmth made a sandwich of themselves by pulling the couch mattress over their bodies and extra pillows over their heads.

The winter was a cold one. One stormy night the wind blew both doors open and while the girls slept snow sifted silently across the floor. By morning a three-foot drift had wafted in, meandering its way "in the back door, through the kitchen and living room and out the front door."

Under such conditions bringing in the wood was even more of a chore than usual. Whether they paid eight dollars a week to buy their own or 'borrowed' from the school's woodpile, it still had to be carried in, especially on washdays when the oil drum heater was kept hot. A large boiler was set on the stove. Water or snow was pailed into it, heated, and washing powder added. Clothes washing was a tedious job done by hand. Thankfully, one of the mothers offered her washing machine to do sheets and towels. Doris and Magdalene were grateful for this generosity. They didn't even have a clothesline. They rigged up what they could with whatever was available and strung their clothes to dry—inside in winter and outside in summer.

By this time the war was over and servicemen were returning home. After their adventures away they were easily bored and hankered for entertainment. Magdalene and others in the community made sure there was always something to do. They played badminton in the hall every night, (twice on Sunday). "Klondike Days", was a popular event, complete with mock sheriff tossing miscreants into the clink for "robbing" the bank. Magdalene's imagination knew no bounds. When a Halloween masquerade was held she dressed up as the Pirate Dundirk of Dowdee, *(". . . was as wicked as wicked could be . . .")*. Everybody thought she was a man. She even flirted with the ladies. None the wiser by the end of the night, they awarded her the men's prize!

When nothing else was happening, the teacherage became the natural meeting place for young adults. Masquerades aside, teachers were expected to be models of propriety. They knew they were being watched and allowed no drinking on the premises. Just how serious they were became clear the night one fellow tried. Magdalene snatched his bottle, broke it and poured the contents down the drain. Then she asked him to leave.

No alcohol didn't mean no fun. The favourite entertainment was Monopoly, a board game that had taken the nation by storm the previous decade. The first round of the evening was pretty friendly, but after that a cutthroat atmosphere prevailed. The gasoline lamp blazed far into the night. As the old school stood on a hill, visible to the entire region, it wasn't long before rumours flew. Without a doubt, wild shenanigans were taking place there all night and the teachers were sleeping it off until noon. Magdalene's approach to these allegations was typical of her approach to life: whenever possible use humour to see you through. One evening she lit the lamp and went to bed, just to amuse herself at the expense of the rumourmongers. The next day she was rewarded by the inquisitive tone of several townspeople as they casually remarked, "My but your light was on late last night!"

"Oh was it?" she smiled. "What time did it go out?"

It was easy for Magdalene not to take offence, for in general the people of the Peace River district were among the finest she'd ever known—kind, generous and hard working.

One returning serviceman was particularly amorous towards Magdalene. He was very handsome, but soon she discovered his real intentions. "He was a wolfhound," she flatly states.

One day, while out in a field gathering potatoes with a friend, Magdalene came across a strangely shaped tuber. It looked like a little man with two arms, a leg and a head. She decided to dress it up like her admirer and have a little fun. She and her friend gave it eyes, nose, mouth, curly wool hair, shirt, pants and necktie. Then they fashioned a bed from a shoebox and placed the doll into it with a note saying: "Does anybody know who I am?" They knew just where to find the rogue. Beer parlors in small towns were always busy. Women were not allowed, but they arranged to have the shoebox placed in the tavern for the young man. Afterward, Magdalene heard what happened from a highly amused patron. The fellow opened the box and was utterly confounded.

"Who did it became the sport of the day!" chuckles Magdalene.

She kept her lips firmly sealed. It wasn't until fifty years later that she finally "admitted to the deed."

"My we laughed over that!"

Even with all the merrymaking Magdalene never forgot her reason for being in Wanham. Her enormous love for children was why she'd become a teacher in the first place. In the northern community she had thirty-five students. When the store brought in a case of Mackintosh toffee—thirty-six bars—she bought the entire thing and before 'coming out' to return to Ponoka for

Christmas, she gave one big bar to each of her students. She, and the toffee, were big hits!

The following year Magdalene advanced to teaching in a school on the outskirts of Edmonton. Conditions were not much better. Her classroom was an old abandoned church with no plumbing. The toilet was a pail in the supply room. Before dumping it out they added ink so it didn't show up yellow in the snow. The high ceilings made the air so cold that the children wore hats, mittens and boots until noon. The stove was inefficient and hazardous. No jacket was in place around it to protect those who came near and to force heat both up to the ceiling and down to the floor. Occasionally carbon pressure built up inside to such a degree that the stove door spontaneously blew open.

Magdalene stayed there two years, after which she and her students moved into the new Forest Heights School. The forties were over for Magdalene, but her adventures had just begun. Over the years she continued to find unique ways to combine her three passions: children, education, and world travel.

October 2000 saw the fruition of yet another dream: the opening of the Me Ai (translation: beautiful child) Training Centre in Chimaltenango, Guatemala. The centre is named in memory of her adopted Korean daughter Me Ai Harder and Me Ai's children (Magdalene's grandchildren) Kristi and Tyler.

"The best week of my life was going down there to the opening," glows Magdalene. "To see all those children and realize that that building was going to make a difference."

Her greatest adventure to date!

Rachel

. . . .
. . . .

 Rachel Rasmussen's high school principal saw something in her that she couldn't. That's why he spent two
classroom periods trying to convince her to become a
teacher. She certainly saw something in *him*. He had a tendency
to use sarcasm and she didn't want to be like that. What's more,
her favourite teacher was an 'old maid' and she didn't want to be
like that either. If that's what the profession did to you she didn't
want any of it!

Then she was asked to instruct the primary class in her
church, and a whole new world opened up to her. Not many people can manage eight rambunctious little boys at once and claim
to enjoy it. Rachel not only enjoyed it, she loved it. A year later
she enrolled without hesitation in the Calgary Normal School.

She calls it "abnormal Normal School."

"There were about 100 girls and ten boys because the rest of
them were in the services," she recalls. "We used to sing the song,
'There Were Ten Pretty Boys at the Normal School'."

Rachel was one of the Normalites who, in 1942, trained and
taught on a rotating basis, attending school for a couple of
months, then teaching for a couple, then returning to school.

"The postmistress in my hometown said, 'If you get a chance
to go out in the first class do it. Then you can come back and get

your questions answered.' We only had August and September training before we went out."

Rachel was assigned the Neutral Hills School in east-central Alberta. It was a long way from her hometown of Magrath in southern Alberta. In fact, to the young girl, it was a long way from everything. Because of train routes and schedules it took two days to get home, requiring an overnight stop in Consort and a jog over to Red Deer before the slow trip south brought her to familiar territory again.

The raucous household in which Rachel boarded was a complete change from the domestic order to which she was accustomed. A great deal of swearing and drinking took place, both of which were wholly foreign to her. Rachel found herself instinctively withdrawing.

"I was so homesick," she remembers. "I spent a lot of my time writing letters to my brothers and friends in the services."

By contrast, Rachel's hosts were very social. A steady stream of visitors appeared at their door at all hours. Rachel still didn't feel included. Even when she tried to help they brushed her aside.

"I would offer to go downstairs to get fruit or something—to help, you know, with the household things. No, they'd never let me go down the stairs."

Rachel felt more and more uncomfortable and isolated. By Christmas she just didn't feel she could stay. A Swedish family offered her a room with them. This was much more to her liking. Among other things, Rachel's background was Scandinavian. She fit right in.

In casual conversation with the people at her new lodgings one day Rachel mentioned what a lot of company her former boarding place had.

"No wonder," came the amused reply. "They have a still in their basement!"

Rachel's eyes popped. It had never occurred to the young innocent that bootlegging was going on beneath her very nose!

School was a place where Rachel was much more in her element even though, like so many others who'd never been in a country school, the concept of many grades in one room was mind-boggling. Rachel soon realized that she was uniquely suited to the job. She had several younger siblings and was quite used to children. Her experience teaching church school was a big help, as was her church experience in general. This became clear the day they had to tell a story to a grade two class as part of practice teaching in Normal School. The diminutive 5'2" Rachel was completely at ease with the assignment while her partner, a far more imposing 5'9", was "scared to death."

"In our church a lot of talks have to be given by the young people," she explains. "I was never so grateful for my training in that."

In January, when Rachel and others who'd gone out were scheduled to return to Normal, they were asked if they'd stay on in their schools until February. To sweeten the deal they were offered a larger allowance for room and board. Rachel remembers that some stayed and some didn't.

"I did because I'd got used to it by then. Then we went back [to Normal School] and finished up for March and April."

Rachel was enormously relieved to be back home. "They offered me a school anywhere in the division when I finished," she remembers, "and I said, 'If I can't get one closer to home I'll quit teaching.'"

The Department of Education was quite willing to accommodate. She got a position in a school in Glenwood, near

Cardston, where she taught grades five and six for two years. During that time she went to summer school to complete her Permanent Teaching Certificate.

Soon afterwards she became Mrs. Lloyd Woodruff. She has lived a rich life, including returning to teaching for twenty-two years. She also raised ten children of her own. "Old maid" indeed!

Pearl

 Pearl Rude jumped in with both feet. After six months of Normal School in Moose Jaw, Saskatchewan she was assigned a school that "had been closed for over a year."

"I started teaching in the Rush Valley S.D. on 9 March 1943 at eighty dollars a month," she remembers. "Most of the pupils had received no instruction whatsoever while the school was closed."

Before she could even begin it was left to the inexperienced girl to determine the grade level of each student, an enormous job made even more difficult by the dearth of textbooks, reference books and updated materials in the school. The superintendent presented himself the first day of classes with the register and "data on the grades" but after that she was on her own.

"It took about a week to get the needed readers, spellers, and so on for each pupil," Pearl recalls. "There was very little money for supplies and I had to make my own seatwork material, flashcards and things of that kind."

The first few days were chaotic. "There wasn't even a clock in the school," she says, "and I had no wristwatch so the first two days we came home an hour late and the next two days . . . an hour early."

Pearl was lucky to have a school close enough for her to

return to her family on weekends. After the first week of confusion she went home Friday night determined to solve the problem. "I borrowed two dollars from my grandfather and bought an alarm clock. After that we got home on time."

Life wasn't all hardship those first few days. Five days after she arrived she was blessed with one of the rarest, most mystical experiences known to humankind. In one breathtakingly magical moment she fell completely and hopelessly in love. Albert Jaster's parents lived in the district but he was stationed with the RCAF in Mossbank, Saskatchewan. They met while he was home on leave and it was abundantly clear that he was equally smitten! They began dating. Pearl's admiration was so firmly fixed that even a major mishap on one of their first dates couldn't put a damper on it. While picking her up in his car one afternoon Albert accidentally rammed the gate of the fence around the school. He knocked it down. As the schoolmistress, Pearl was responsible and she found herself in very hot water! It wasn't comfortable for the nineteen-year-old but, as all things do, the incident eventually blew over. Before long Pearl was proving herself worthy of praise.

One thing affecting her deeply was the privation her sixteen students had undergone as victims of the depression.

"My pupils had had no opportunity to visit any cities or learn about anything that happened outside their district. I tried to bring a little happiness into their lives through singing, art work, games and especially reading books such as *Tom Sawyer, Huckleberry Finn, Little Women*, and the Laura Ingalls Wilder books which I was able to borrow from the library in Herbert."

The depression was still keenly felt in the Rush Lake area. It took farmers a long time to get back on their feet after ten years of drought and rock bottom grain prices. The family with whom Pearl boarded was no exception.

"Their farmhouse consisted of a lean-to kitchen, front room and two bedrooms. However, one bedroom had been turned into a storage room for wheat. That room had to be cleaned out for the children and I was given the parents' bedroom."

Almost universally in schools across the prairies the biggest event of the year was the Christmas concert. Everyone in the district attended in their best attire to watch the children perform and visit with 'Santa', who produced gifts and candy bags for all of them. Afterwards a lunch was served, courtesy of the ladies, who brought sandwiches, cakes and cookies. Coffee was brewed in a large wash boiler on the school stove. With desks pushed to the walls, dancing commenced, often until dawn. "Visiting went on and on," remembers Shirley (Magee) McKibbin warmly, "while the little ones slept on piles of coats and jackets." It was an event the entire district looked forward to all year. For better or for worse, a teacher's worth was often judged by the calibre of concert he or she produced.

Pearl found herself in a bind as concert time approached. The money to finance a proper one simply wasn't there. She thought long and hard and finally came up with a plan.

"I got the older boys to make wooden toys and the girls made tea towels, pot holders, etc. by hand. A month before Christmas we had a dance and auction sale. We took in nineteen dollars, a lot of money then. We were able to buy a box of apples, oranges, candy, a tree (we borrowed decorations), and a small gift for each child. We were able to have our Christmas concert and had a dance after as well."

The evening was memorable in more ways than one. The sparkle in the children's eyes was soon outdone by the sparkle in Pearl's own. Albert presented her with a diamond engagement ring!

"We were married on 8 April 1944," she smiles. "I continued teaching until June 30 and I moved to Mossbank to be with my husband."

Her time in the Rush Valley S.D. was very well spent. "It was a hard struggle for me and my students," she frankly states, "but in the sixteen months I taught there I put most of them through two years' work. During those sixteen months we had only three weeks holidays as well."

Verla

. . . .
. . . .

 Pearl (Rude) Jaster was out teaching after six months of Normal School, but she could've been out much earli-er. After six weeks of training she and her fellow Normalites were tested and those with the highest marks were offered schools on the spot.

"I could have gone to the Meadow Lake area," she remem-bers, "but my father wanted me to continue my training."

Pearl took the Rush Valley School a mere four and a half months later only because it was an opportunity to teach five miles from her home.

Verla Lavachek (now Nevay) was one Normalite who took advantage of the chance to teach after six weeks of training, but her school was nowhere near her central Saskatchewan roots. To get to the Bluebell area in northwestern Saskatchewan she took a bus from Rosetown to Saskatoon, then to North Battleford, then to Meadow Lake. In Meadow Lake the people she was to board with picked her up and took her a further thirty miles to their home. By this time Verla felt completely alone and cut off from the world that she knew.

In 1943 there were no roads to speak of in the wooded area northwest of Meadow Lake—just crude trails. The Wilroy School sat surrounded by trees and brush. The first day Verla arrived early.

As 9:00 AM approached she stared in fascination (and a touch of alarm) as thirty-six students appeared, one at a time, as if from nowhere out of the bush. She states unequivocally that making it through that day was the biggest accomplishment of her life.

Verla soon discovered that the people in the district were so poor they couldn't pay their school taxes. That meant Verla herself did not get paid. She immediately went into arrears on her room and board and was so strapped she had to borrow money from her father to buy the coat and overshoes she badly needed for a northern Saskatchewan winter.

Verla felt she had little choice but to persevere. As she grew accustomed to the situation she realized that despite the drawback of no pay she liked the people and enjoyed the school and the children. Only one unpleasant incident marred her time there. In those days rural schools had barns for the horses students often rode or drove to school. The barn was a favourite hangout, especially for boys, whose fondness for clandestine activities was unsurpassed. When trustees learned that some boys were sneaking tobacco to school and smoking it in the barn they demanded that Verla administer the strap. She was mortified. She'd heard stories of teachers who were hated because they used the strap. Reluctantly she did as she was told.

"Each whack hurt me more than it did the kids," she grimaces.

Another thing that horrified her was stories of teachers who broke rulers over the children. Verla made every effort to avoid both the strap and the ruler. The fact that she "loved all [her] kids" probably accounts for her statement that she never had many discipline problems.

Even though she enjoyed teaching, Verla knew by Christmas that she'd leave the Wilroy School. She simply couldn't continue to work for nothing. First, however, there was the Christmas Concert to produce.

It was quite a challenge to find parts for thirty-six students, but not as much of a worry as the stage curtains turned out to be. Sheets were the preference in most rural schools. They were usually borrowed from the mother of one of the students. To have one's sheets on display was a major affair. Emilia (Vogel) Raab calls to mind that "there were always a few mothers who claimed their sheets were whiter. They always pointed out which was theirs." It was a matter of honour to have title to the whitest sheets in the district.

Verla had not yet found curtains for her stage when, a few days before the concert, she received a strange note. It read:

"Miss Verla teacher, I am borrow two sheets for the xmas concert, but if you make them dirty, you have to come and wash them here. If not, I come get you with the strap."

It was signed *"Your sweetheart"* by a man who lived near the school. Verla was disconcerted. She'd never met the man and was uncertain what to make of the note. When she asked the older girls about him they assured her that he was a good sort—just a bit of a character. So she decided to take him up on his offer.

The concert went well, other than Verla trying her utmost to keep the sheets clean for fear of the consequences. In those days, like Pearl's dance and auction sale, money was raised for the children's gifts and candy by holding special district events. Socials in which pies or fancy boxed lunches were auctioned off were favourites. Emilia remembers that for a basket social "the ladies would make a nicely decorated basket of lunch [no one knew whose it was]. They were raffled to the highest bidder." Dances and card parties were also popular.

The teacher often used the money raised to place a catalogue order to the T. Eaton Company. She included the name of each child beside the item selected for him or her. Before long a parcel arrived bearing the gifts already wrapped and tagged for the individual children. Santa distributed these at the concert. Verla recalls that the jolly old elf often found a gift for the teacher too, but was not forthcoming with it until he received a kiss. She wonders what the male teachers did, since Mrs. Claus rarely travelled.

The day after the Wilroy concert, Verla left for home. She was disillusioned with teaching—not because she didn't like it. She couldn't afford it! Before she left the district did come up with what they owed her, but once she paid off her room and board she had only $154.

Verla had all but decided to give up on the profession when a position came open in the Austin School very near her home. That meant she could save money by staying with her grandmother who lived only half a mile from the school. She was back in business!

"January 1944 to December 1944 I was paid $638.34," she states. "January to December 1945 I was paid $804.10."

Things were definitely improving!

Then in January 1946 Verla applied to the Edward Lake School in the Medstead area of Saskatchewan. She was in for a rude surprise.

She arrived to begin teaching February 5 only to discover that there had been no school held at all that year. Verla had five months to get thirty-plus students through a whole year's work! A less intrepid soul would have quit on the spot. Instead, Verla went into action.

"My students were anxious to get their year's work done," she says.

She asked permission of the parents to work with the younger children during the day and have the older students stay until six o'clock so she could work with them later. What ensued was five months of intense effort. In order to get all the material covered there was no time to take notes or delve into textbooks. Verla stood before the students and delivered instruction orally. Amazingly, it worked. In June everybody passed. Despite the pressure of a tight deadline, everybody working together generated a happy atmosphere. This was Verla's favourite school.

"I stayed on another year with this fine bunch of children," she says. "Each year I got a bit of a raise so I was quite happy."

Verla did all of this on six weeks of training and a Temporary Teaching Certificate. She was supposed to have gone back to Normal School to get her First Class Certificate, but her inspector was happy with her work and each year a letter arrived saying her Temporary Certificate had been renewed.

Finally, after Edward Lake she went back and achieved her First Class Interim Teaching Certificate. But four years had taken their toll. Verla was exhausted and left on a deserved holiday. On returning, renewed and raring to go, she received a visit from trustees of yet another school unit. She'd been recommended for the Wiggins school in the Herschel district. Off and running again!

"I taught at Wiggins School in the Rosetown School Unit for a year," she states. "In July 1948 I married Leonard McLellan. We lived in Valley Center, Saskatchewan and I did some spare teaching in that area. My greatest moment was when I went back to teach as a spare in 1949 at Marriott School, and I stood up at the front of my class saying the Lord's Prayer, saluting the flag and singing 'O Canada.' I hoped that my special teacher, Mrs. Christensen, was looking down—as she taught me from grade three right through to grade nine in that very same school!"

Frances

. . . .
. . . .

The war was still in its infancy when Frances Ost left home to attend Normal School in 1940. She was a first-generation Canadian with Norwegian and Prussian roots, but her name was too suspiciously German for the comfort of many. Anti-German sentiment ran so high that it was easy to transpose it onto anyone with even remotely German connections. Despite her volunteer work as a junior hostess for servicemen at both the Salvation Army and the Roman Catholic Church, Frances soon sensed that something was wrong.

It was the little things. Not getting an invitation to a class party, and being relegated to the poorest ball team at a Sports Day even though she was an ace pitcher. Then a more sinister pattern emerged. In some subjects she received consistently poor marks, but when outside people who didn't know her were asked to judge the students (army officers in the case of Physical Education), she was graded second highest in the class.

One instructor "openly showed me his dislike," Frances remembers. She failed an assignment she had spent the weekend diligently working on. "My roommate didn't read the book. [She] had me tell her enough for six lines. [She] passed."

Frances got the message. She was boarding off-campus and for the duration of the year "kept a reserved distance from [the school] at every opportunity." Graduation was a cause for celebration!

Frances didn't care to repeat any negative experiences so when she learned that the school she was offered near Dunmore, Alberta was "ripped apart by dissension," she turned it down. The next school, in a German district south of Burdett, was much more to her liking, but it fell through as well. After she accepted it a teacher shuffle due to problems with another school put Frances, finally, at the Morning Star School southeast of Grassy Lake.

Unfortunately, things didn't go smoothly there either.

"I was told I shouldn't have told the parents I had German blood," she relates.

It was frightening at the best of times for a young teacher to be all alone in a strange situation. A show of friendship was extremely important and could make or break a teacher's stay, or even a career. On the first Sunday Frances was at Morning Star a church service was held in the school. In most districts it was customary for the teacher to be invited afterwards to someone's home for Sunday dinner. Frances was ignored.

As difficult as that was, it was better than what happened a short while later.

"One family promised to include me to attend a show on a Friday night," she remembers. "They drove off before the time I was to meet them."

Frances was bitterly hurt. Tears soaked her pillow that night, but comfort was on its way. A strange sixth sense brought her parents to her teacherage door the next morning. They were happy to see their daughter, but shocked at the one-room hovel she lived in. It didn't even have a bed. Frances had to purchase a folding couch to sleep on.

"To survive, my parents bought me a gas stove, a gas iron, a gas lamp and food. My first cheque was sixty-three dollars—raise at Christmas. [I] got about $750 for a year."

As gas was crucial to keep army vehicles and equipment running during the war, it was strictly rationed on the home front. Rural schools didn't need lighting during the day, but if an event was held in the evening residents of the district brought gas lanterns from home to light the school.

In December word came from the school division that in order to conserve gas there were to be no Christmas concerts that year. The district was up in arms and Frances was caught in the middle. A delegation of ladies came to her and insisted she hold a concert. What could she do? She tried to appease both sides by arranging a small concert, then withdrawing.

"[I] prepared a few items, people met, I went home."

She was glad she did. Even though alcohol was rationed too, it seemed in plentiful supply. At some point in the evening a few men were feeling sufficiently merry to "shoot up a telephone pole" in the schoolyard.

In January Frances came down with quinsy, a nasty, extremely painful complication of severe tonsillitis. Again she realized the coolness towards her. Not a soul came to check on her or express their concern—unusual at a time when neighbourliness was taken for granted.

The teacherage was unbearable to live in. It was so small and poorly constructed that "if the stove was lit it was too hot, and if the stove went out water froze in the kettle." Frances packed up and moved across the road. There she "washed floors, dishes, baked cakes, ironed clothes," and performed other duties in exchange for room and board, until spring arrived and she could move to the teacherage again.

The following year, 1942, Frances took a position teaching grades five to eight in Duchess, Alberta. She remembers that she got the job "when an employee in the school office wanted a female to chum with."

Some time after she arrived the principal of the school enlisted in the armed forces. The primary teacher followed suit. Frances herself seriously considered leaving to take on another career, but was foiled when all teaching jobs were frozen in 1943.

Nevertheless, she nearly ended up with no school to teach in that year. It all started when she noticed how dirty her classroom floor was. She decided to have a clean-up day.

"The girls mopped [the school]," she explains. "The boys raked the yard and piled the grass. I lit the bonfire. God provided the whirlwind. We had ourselves a fire that threatened destruction of the school!"

In panic they dashed for the water the girls were using on the floor. To their enormous relief, it was just enough to put out the flames.

Flames of a different sort were smoldering elsewhere.

"There was discrimination," Frances relates, "but not from the element one might expect. It was an Italian-Canadian who was going to rub me out. Her girls had spread a nasty rumour about a classmate. I spoke to the girls. The mother took exception to my words. She headed to the schoolyard, but stopped at the gate and reconsidered the matter. I'm glad she did as I'd done heavy farm work and wouldn't have allowed her to harm me without stiff resistance."

Frances recalls another, less threatening, but no less unsettling incident. She boarded with the station agent. One Saturday afternoon he suggested she attend a church tea.

"With gloves and hat and all I went over alone. Outside the

church property on the sidewalk I found a five dollar bill. Wow! In ecstasy I told the ladies. 'It's ours' (they curtly responded). 'Church property.' I lost my goldmine."

The inspector for the Duchess School was impressed with Frances' work and hired her the following year to teach grades seven and eight in Bassano—the classes his children were in. Frances was delighted, but before she left Duchess there was one parting shot.

"Someone stole all my boxed books on [my] last night in town."

Bassano appeared to be a much more promising situation. It was conveniently located on bus and train routes so Frances could get home on weekends. She liked the town and the people and found the school children studious and well behaved. She even met a "gentleman friend" who waited for her at the school gate each day and walked her home for lunch.

"Home" was another boarding place and therein lay the only shortcoming. Frances couldn't handle eating liver every single day. After two months of it, she moved out.

"Then the inspector's friend found out I was of German extraction," she states. Things began to deteriorate.

First of all one of the inspector's children started showing up late for school and was sent home by Frances for refusing to abide by school rules. People found this quite amusing at the inspector's expense. Then Frances accused his other child of breaking a window. The inspector was livid, but Frances wouldn't back down. A "battle royal" ensued. In the end Frances tendered her resignation. She'd gone up against the big guns and was sure she'd be dismissed from teaching.

But fortune was her friend. She took a chance on applying for a job teaching grade nine and ten at the Collegiate Institute in Lethbridge, considered at the time to be the best high school in southern Alberta. To her astonishment she was hired.

"I was in heaven," she recalls. "That is until the staff discovered I was not degreed (and) requested my dismissal."

The board was reluctant to let her go. Instead they transferred her the following year to another school in which she taught half days and supervised the rest.

"That job lasted from the Tuesday after Labour Day to Thursday," she laughs. "My grade nine test results were excellent. Back to LCI!"

Frances taught until February 1948 when at her father's behest she requested immediate leave to take her ailing brother to the Mayo Clinic in Rochester. Once again she thought she'd be permanently let go, but she wasn't. Her father himself was so ill he wasn't expected to live past the summer. At the end of the school year Frances reluctantly resigned.

Despite the barriers Frances faced because of her heritage at a time when tolerance was almost non-existent, she advanced from teaching in a rural one-room school to a city high school in a mere ten years. Ironically, it is the characteristics of her ethnicity— the very thing that would have held her back—that actually saw her through. John Charyk, in his book *Those Bittersweet School Days*, suggests that "the Russians and Germans were a sturdy race, hard working and thrifty." Frances herself adds to that with "serious achievers, honesty coupled with industry."

Frances went on to earn two university degrees and in 1974 was offered a fellowship for doctoral students at the University of British Columbia. She taught until 1984. A long and distinguished career!

Ruby

Shortly after the year began at Kingsley School in the Somerset district of Manitoba in 1943, eighteen-year-old Ruby Plomp (now Anderson) added one more student to her class. A fifteen-year-old girl taking grade ten by correspondence.

"I was asked if I would help her if needed, mark her two-week tests and mail her monthly tests to the Department of Education," says Ruby. "Little did I know how much help she would need or how busy I would be with my [eleven other students in six grades]."

Despite the extra effort demanded, the girl turned out to be a gift. With so little age difference between them, teacher and student developed a fast friendship, a common consequence of those times.

"Often I helped [her] after school or in the evenings. In turn, she helped me in various ways. She often listened to the younger children read, drilled them on arithmetic facts or heard their spelling words."

Ruby was a permit teacher with only six weeks of training, the equivalent of what today amounts to merely the introductory weeks of a four-year university degree. She faced a huge amount of work, often staying at school well past dismissal time, marking assignments and preparing the next day's lessons. Every two months, when all grades were tested for report cards, she carried on late into the night, developing exams and marking them by lamplight in her boarding house bedroom. It frustrated her that the days never seemed long enough to get through all the planned material. Soon, like a fully trained teacher, she learned to combine grades in subjects such as Health and Nature Study, but she still worried that there wasn't enough time to finish the year's work. Her anxiety was heightened by several school closures due to storms, and one horrific week when the school closed because most of the children (and Ruby herself) contracted scabies, an itchy, highly contagious rash. After that Ruby and the children doubled their efforts and did indeed get the work done, although Ruby says, "The year went by too quickly for me."

The children were unaware of how much extra work Ruby did. They only knew they liked her. Ruby ate her lunch with them, out in the schoolyard if the weather was fine.

"The children begged me to join them for games after lunch and at recess. I usually did, although often my mind was on the next lessons to be taught."

Just before Thanksgiving Ruby attended the annual Teachers' Convention in Killarney. It was well worth the bus trip.

"How encouraging and helpful to share in groups with other permit teachers!" she exclaims. "Each one's situation was different but we were able to compare and get ideas from each other. Leading other sessions were experienced teachers ready to answer our many questions."

Ruby made good use of all the advice she received. The inspector turned up twice during the year and found no fault with what he saw. He assured Ruby she was doing a good job.

By spring she was comfortable and confident in her role. She took on two more charges with ease.

"There was no kindergarten at that time, but five-year-olds were allowed to attend school from Easter until June," she explains. "Two little boys joined us. I prepared seatwork for them and older pupils helped them with paperwork."

Also in the spring, forms arrived for her from the Department of Education in Winnipeg. It was time to fulfill the terms of the agreement she had signed to attend Normal School when her teaching permit expired. Ruby filled out the application. By this time she knew beyond a doubt that she had chosen the right career.

Teaching wasn't all that was expected of a rural educator. Often the janitor work was left to him or her as well. Ruby enlisted the help of her friend, the grade ten girl, to share the chore.

"Before winter firewood was stacked in the basement. Storm windows were put up. We learned how to get fires going in the heater and the furnace."

Ruby remembers every detail of her little one-room school.

"It had a small porch with coat hooks on two walls. A shelf across one corner held a large crock for drinking water. Beside it was a wash basin and soap. The classroom had rows of desks of various sizes, the first row having double desks for the youngest pupils. On one side of the room were four long narrow windows. Another window was at the back. All had white, tieback frilled curtains. Blackboards ran along the opposite side and across the front of the room. A large teacher's desk and swivel chair sat at the front. Nearby was an old piano. At the back of the room was a wood-burning heater and a large cupboard which was the library. A framed picture of the King and Queen, and Red Cross posters adorned the walls. A Union Jack flag stood in the corner, ready to be hoisted on the flagpole outdoors when school was in progress. A door led to the basement. In it was a furnace and pile of wood and some coal. Behind a curtained-off corner sat a chemical toilet, for winter use . . . as there were two outside toilets. Near them was a small horse barn."

For one day in both the fall and the spring Ruby got all the students involved in a thorough school cleaning.

"Walls were dusted, pictures cleaned, piano carefully dusted and windows washed inside and out. Curtains were sent home with older students to be washed. I volunteered to iron them. The board floor was scrubbed and oiled. How proud we all were of our clean school!"

Ruby was happy to help out at her boarding place too. She stayed in the beautiful farm home of the school board secretary. His family immediately put her at ease, making it clear that her family and friends were welcome anytime as well. Ruby especially appreciated the lady of the house who was once a schoolteacher herself.

"She was a great help and always an encouragement to me," she remembers. "Sometimes after the children were in bed we ironed clothes, one at each end of the long kitchen table. We used sad irons, heated on the large wood-burning kitchen range. She would relate stories from her teaching days."

Ruby paid twenty dollars a month room and board from her paycheque of $63.15. As she helped more and more around the house, however, her landlady reduced that to fifteen dollars.

"This was a help to me," she says, "as for some months I was paying five dollars out of each cheque on a second-hand bicycle I had bought for riding home [twelve miles] on weekends."

The people of the district received Ruby warmly. It wasn't long before she felt as though she'd been born there.

"Like other teachers before me, I was invited to the various homes for a meal, a night, and sometimes a weekend."

She joined the Ladies' Aid and enjoyed the camaraderie experienced as they carried out their many projects for the war, writing letters to servicemen, assembling care packages and raising money for the Red Cross.

Young people were always welcome at her boarding place and often came over to join Ruby, the farm's hired man, and the hired girl on the homemade skating rink they "all helped to make between the house and barn."

"For a winter evening of fun we bundled into a high-box with loose straw in the bottom," she fondly remembers. "Pulled by a team of horses and 'laughing all the way' we rode into Somerset or Swan-Lake. We called these outings 'Tally-Ho's'. We skated or bowled or occasionally attended a movie. Before heading home we hoped we could find a restaurant open."

There was only one drawback to Ruby's year at Kingsley: she grew to love the children and the community. As the end of the school year approached she dreaded leaving.

"I would gladly have stayed if the Department of Education had permitted. On the final afternoon a school picnic was held. We all enjoyed games and races. Parents joined us, bringing lunch and homemade ice cream. The Chairman of the Board thanked me for a job well done and extended best wishes from all. The pupils gave me gifts and hugs. Leaving was not easy. The year I spent at Kingsley was, in retrospect, one of the busiest, happiest years of my life!"

Claudia

. . . .
. . . .

 Leonard Wold remembers 1944 as the year the pretty young supervisor came to oversee the Leopoldville School near Alliance, Alberta. His own school, Norway, had closed the year before with students given a choice of either home study or studying under a supervisor in the next district. Leonard, a grade nine student, decided to go to Leopoldville in hopes that the schoolhouse atmosphere would help provide a more structured study environment.

Claudia Elm (now Williams) was recruited through her high school to supervise at Leopoldville. She had just graduated from grade twelve in her home school several miles away.

"It was too far to commute," she remembers, "so I had to board. I had nine students. I saw they got their lessons done and helped them when necessary. I don't remember any problems with the kids."

But Leonard does. A few of the boys were real cut-ups. Of course they always made sure Miss Elm was not around when they threw twenty-two calibre shotgun shells into the hot stove.

"It sounded like war," grins Leonard, (appropriate at a time when war games were the order of the day for almost every schoolboy). "The bigger the bang the better the thrill!"

The school was left unlocked so that students arriving early could find shelter in poor weather. A perfect opportunity for mayhem! One day "things got carried away," Leonard remembers, "and there was some damage done to the school." Fortunately the janitor, a fellow from a farm nearby, "arrived on the scene and laid the law down." By the time Claudia got there it was all over.

Two of the boys were particular bullies. Their special delight was coercing three young sisters into stealing tobacco from their father and bringing it to school. The boys needed something to smoke! The girls were terrified. If they didn't oblige they'd get "beat up." They did as they were ordered. It didn't save one of them, however, from further torment. She was reduced to tears one day when her textbook was confiscated and "made a mess of." According to Leonard the boys did that "just to add some excitement to their day."

Claudia was unaware of the trouble. She had her hands full looking after the students during school hours.

"We all had lunch there and played ball and games at recess and noons."

Claudia often thought of her sister as she packaged up the completed lessons to send to the Correspondence School Branch of the Department of Education in Edmonton. Catherine worked there, receiving the lessons, processing them for marking, typing and illustrating new lessons and sending out courses to students, supervisors, and men and women in the services.

Claudia longed for the companionship that Catherine enjoyed with the girls who worked in the Correspondence School Branch office.

"I was quite lonesome, my first time away from home and no young people around."

Perhaps Claudia didn't notice that there were indeed one or

two young people around and they seemed especially interested in her! Leonard knew of two boys who had heavy crushes on the young supervisor. He remembers one in particular who showed up during school hours and caused a general distraction. You couldn't blame the boys. Claudia was a sweet girl. She drew suitors like bees to honey.

She didn't stick around to satisfy their interest though. She was anxious to go home on weekends and that she did, even though it meant parting with some pay to help cover the gas it cost her father to drive out and pick her up.

Claudia remembers two highlights from her year at Leopoldville. Both were disruptions of the normal routine. One was exceedingly pleasant; the other sheer horror.

A wonderful break came when supervisors from the entire region were invited to attend a teachers' convention in Camrose.

"It was all very exciting," she declares.

The animosity some teachers felt towards the 'sitters' was either well hidden, or Claudia chose to ignore it. She had a lovely time, due in part to the very rare treat of restaurant dinners and hotel lodgings. The dance that capped off the convention was a perfect climax to the event.

Back in Leopoldville it was business as usual, until the day Claudia looked out the window to see a frightening sight. Smoke and flames were licking their way towards the school! It was a huge prairie fire! In one heart-stopping moment she realized they were trapped.

"The roads home for the kids were in the line of fire," she quivers to recall.

By now the rest of the children were aware of what was going on.

"We were all pretty scared," she remembers. But Claudia

knew that as the one in charge she must remain calm. Quickly she assessed the situation. There was a field they could get to that had been tilled black. No fire could reach them there. In haste she herded the children out the door and into the field. There they huddled until help arrived.

Fortunately, the school was not lost and the children, though badly frightened, were safe.

At the end of the year Leopoldville School closed its doors for the last time, just as Norway School had done the year before. The school consolidation becoming more and more prevalent because of teacher shortages and diminishing rural populations necessitated Leonard and the others being bussed to school in Alliance.

Claudia's stint as a supervisor was over. She had no desire to carry on.

"I left and went to Edmonton where I got a job with the Income Tax," she states.

Claudia doesn't remember how much money she made as a supervisor, but it's a safe bet it was far less than what she made in her next job!

Pat

. . . .

. . . .

 When Siama Mattson left her family's farm near Three Hills, Alberta to teach in the Little Gem district near Veteran the first thing that changed was her name.

"Siama?! What kind of a name is that?" teased a brash young man from nearby Hemaruka. "I'm going to call you Pat!"

It stuck. From that day forward she was known by one and all as Pat. It was 1937, two years before the war began. The heavy hand of the depression had not yet lifted from the devastated prairies. Pat boarded with the Schetzsles (pronounced like pretzels). They were a large family of seven children crowded into a four-room farmhouse.

"I slept with one of the girls in a bedroom that had two beds in it," she remembers, "and somebody must have slept on the couch. Francis was the oldest. I think there was some kind of a shack so he slept out there. I don't know how we managed when I think about it now."

At the Lothian School Pat had ten students. In retrospect she wonders at conditions there as well.

"The facilities in those country schools! How did we manage? There were the toilets, and nobody cleaned them out in the wintertime when there was a bunch of snow. It's a wonder we didn't perish. But everybody was the same."

For all its necessity the "little house out back" was a sanitation nightmare. Regulations stressed that galvanized buckets be installed beneath the seat holes to collect waste, and flap doors be built into the outhouse rear for ease of the bucket's removal and dumping. In reality most privies were set above a trench and simply moved over a new one when the opening became full. The dirt dug from the new trench was used to cover the old. Even if the job could be done in the winter it was too easy to put off and some pits overflowed.

Snow easily drifted into these tiny houses, sometimes building up as high as the seat. Children who were reluctant to apply warm bottoms to cold benches often "missed" the target. Not wanting to tarry any longer than necessary in sub-zero temperatures—and for other obvious reasons—their "leavings" were usually left untouched, quickly freezing into a solid mass of refuse. Needless to say, students in rural schools tried valiantly not to use the facilities until they could return home at night.

Pat summoned her pupils into school with a handbell. It had been mended so many times that few original parts remained. The handle was a screwdriver and the clapper a large bolt! Such modifications were taken for granted at a time when wasting anything was unthinkable and buying new out of the question.

Pat taught at Lothian for three years before moving on to the Stella School where her class size doubled to twenty-one. Two years later she returned to Little Gem to marry Francis. The little house she first boarded in now became her home.

By this time the war was well underway. Francis, having turned twenty-one, was summoned to Camrose for mandatory basic training. Men who were needed to run family farms were exempt from compulsory military service but Francis was called because it was assumed his father was taking care of the operation. By now, however, Mr. Schetzsle had moved to nearby Naco, helping to make ends meet for his large family by running a garage. He was a skilled mechanic and soon proved himself invaluable to the small community. With Francis gone there was nobody to manage the farm and when Naco realized they were about to lose their mechanic they took action. Petitions circulated calling for Francis to be released from the services.

In the meantime, also to help make ends meet, Pat took the position of schoolmistress at Marby, a rural school about ten miles from their farm. She and her infant son moved into the teacherage there.

"It was just like a little granary," she shivers. Among other things it was "freezing cold!"

It was a miserable winter. One night Pat got the scare of her life.

"I heard a noise. Something going around and around the teacherage."

She was petrified. What, or who, could possibly be out there—miles from nowhere? She was too frightened even to venture a look. She lay stiff and unmoving in her bed for what seemed like hours until, finally, sleep possessed her.

"The next morning here I found some cows in the yard," she states with dismay. It might have been funny if the terror of the night before hadn't taken such a dreadful toll.

The following year, 1943, Pat returned to the farm. The Lothian School needed a teacher once again but pupil numbers had dwindled. Pat received special permission from the superintendent to teach the children at the farm.

"There was a little shack in the yard and that's where I taught," she remembers. "They fixed a blackboard up but [we] didn't have much. We just had a bookcase at Lothian School. All the books to read were . . . in that bookcase; that's all they had. They moved the desks from Lothian out to the farm. Maybe there weren't more than six kids."

With a young baby it was a great help to be able to teach at home, and the children enjoyed the novelty of coming to school on a farm.

"We had some sheep," laughs Pat, "and one boy at recess would like to chase the billy-goat!"

Soon Francis was indeed released from the services and he and Pat began to add to their family.

"I had four children—bang, bang, bang," says Pat, "and I taught pretty well all the time." Later they were blessed with two more.

After her year of teaching in the farmyard, Pat and the students of Lothian all transferred to the school in Hemaruka. She was there three years, first as a teacher, then as teaching principal in the newer three-room school.

While school was in session Pat and her children moved into the teacherage at Hemaruka.

"It wasn't much of a teacherage," she comments, "but better than the one at Marby."

One of her husband's aunts looked after the children during the day, then brought them to school for Pat to take home with her at dismissal time. This was a perfect arrangement as Aunt Olga was also the janitor at the school. Her duties began when Pat's ended.

In 1947 Pat moved up to the vice-principalship of the Veteran School where she also taught grade ten, eleven and some grade twelve courses. This time she didn't have to live in a teacherage. She, her husband and family moved right into town.

Pat taught a total of thirty-three and a half years, retiring in

1976. In the year of Canada's 100th birthday, 1967, she took on a special Centennial project. Thirty years after graduating from a one-year Normal School program she went back to school to earn a Bachelor of Education degree.

"I thoroughly loved teaching school," she exclaims. "I did— or I would never have done it as long as I did!"

Helen

Night after night Helen Simons went to bed crying. It was her first teaching job and everything around her was foreign: the people, the landscape, the one-room country school.

Except for her year at the Edmonton Normal School, eighteen-year-old Helen had never been away from home. The big house surrounded by trees in Fort Saskatchewan was now a distant memory, swallowed up by the flat, featureless prairie east of Three Hills. She'd never even seen a hailstorm!

How would she manage? There was so much to learn. And those great big grade nine boys! They were bound to be trouble for sure. Would she ever get them ready for departmental exams? If only she could just give up and go home!

But Helen knew she couldn't. The people of the district were counting on her. In fact, they looked *up* to her. The *parents* looked up to *her*! She was the schoolteacher. They expected her to be the one with all the answers. Slowly Helen realized how much help they needed and a sense of determination came upon her.

"I needed to make myself live up to their expectations," she avows.

Helen also needed a lot of confidence and says she grew up fast. "All those teachers had to." After a while she was too busy for homesickness. Alberta Teachers' Association meetings once a month helped. They brought colleagues together to share and commiserate and she realized that she wasn't really so alone.

Helen's school was on the edge of a Mennonite settlement and about half of her students were Mennonite. The Mennonites were pacifists and did not involve themselves in the war. She remembers them as so quiet and well behaved that they kept the rest of the class toned down, so she didn't have many discipline problems after all. She also recalls their playful sense of humour. They loved to try to trick her into revealing her age. She never did, perhaps because she was a bit abashed. The Mennonite girls seemed so mature. She remembers the grade nine girls as "more ladylike" than she was, to the extent that when the inspector came he mistook one of them for the teacher!

Helen had a special interest in music and was anxious to enter her students in the music festival at Olds. A potential problem came up when she realized that while the Mennonite children were allowed to sing, they weren't allowed to sing to music. This didn't stymie her for long. The school didn't have a piano or organ anyway. Helen simply taught them to sing acappella. When they arrived at the music festival they were offered accompaniment by the organizers. Of course they had to turn it down. Nevertheless, the students delivered an admirable performance even though, remembers Helen with a smile, they sang one verse in a different key.

Helen worked under a small school board in a close, tightly knit community. At the tail end of the depression in 1940 the people of Helen's district didn't have much. But they strove to support the education of their children. When the grade nine students decided they wanted to learn to type, somehow the district came up with a typewriter.

Helen did her best too. There was no library at the school so for Christmas she bought each child a different book in hopes that they'd share. She remembers giving the older girls books from the *Anne of Green Gables* series and the younger girls *Nancy Drew* books.

Almost every rural school had a Junior Red Cross Club. It convened every Friday afternoon and was often anticipated as the highlight of the week. (When Verla Nevay was a student her mother could keep her home to dig potatoes Thursday, but never, never on a Friday afternoon!) The main purpose of the club was to teach the students about citizenship and health. They elected an executive, conducted meetings and kept records of minutes and financial statements. They raised money and performed activities for various goodwill projects locally and abroad. Debates and public speaking events were staged and it was exciting to write to penpals from Junior Red Cross organizations throughout the world. Each member received a card to check daily for such health habits as clean hands, face, teeth, etc. Certificates of merit were awarded monthly for completed checklists. Each member was also proud to receive a pin with a red cross on it and a regular edition of the Junior Red Cross magazine.

Among other activities Helen's students put together scrapbooks to send to children in hospital in Calgary. With the help of the parents they also made quilts.

After her first year of teaching Helen returned to Normal School for the summer, then taught a second year before receiving her Permanent Certificate.

No longer was she the frightened young girl who was so overwhelmed by her first teaching position. She taught in various schools until 1947, when she married Peter Tainsh, a fellow she'd met while east of Three Hills. Five sons later she went back to teaching, a poised, confident mentor who'd learned a few things along her way. Among them was the role reversal a good teacher often perceives. She attests:

"Teaching is as much for us [the teachers] as it is for them [the students]."

Hazel

· ·
· · · · · · · · · · · · · · · · · ·

 "If I ever get out of here I'm never going to want to see another school again."

Those were the words of Hazel Green (now Smith) while working as a permit teacher in Manitoba in 1942. Hazel lasted one term, from August until Christmas. Excerpts from further letters paint a picture of what it was like for a young girl away from home in charge of a country school:

August 25—Well, I've got my first day over. There were only four children at school . . . [out of an enrolment of ten] . . . We started off by singing "O Canada." It was mostly a solo of poor singing. Then I gave the kids the list of books that they needed. After that I gave them everything I could think of to keep them busy. I am starting school at 9:30 and only having an hour for noon. During the noon hour I swept the place out. It certainly needed it. After that I tidied up the library. I think with some time spent on it I will get it fit to live in . . . We killed a mouse in the school today. A good start.

By the end of the week Hazel was settling in, but so were the first stirrings of uneasiness. She held them bravely at bay.

Friday, 5:30—Well I've got my first week over. I have had only four pupils all week . . . I give them plenty to do and the time passes quickly . . . My school certainly is dirty and small. They are going to have some painting done soon. How are the chances of getting home next weekend—good I'm hoping. The B.'s are very good to me so far. I don't like taking lunch (in a kit) much, but I can put up with a lot when I think of my salary [$700 per year]. I get fairly good meals and lunches.

By mid-September Hazel was happy with the way things were going at school. She felt ambivalent, however, about the hours she spent at 'home'.

September 11—I have had four pupils on the average this week. Shepherds stayed home to help with the threshing and Gordon B. had a spot of impetigo on his leg. Mrs. B. is very careful with it. She keeps it clean and she got some of that ointment that you are supposed to use. I don't think that there is much danger of it spreading . . . When I come home from school now I change into my red slacks (legs rolled up), my blue ship blouse, my old shoes, and those navy socks. I always feel much better and more at home in them. If any-one came I could always change . . . I really enjoy coming home from school and not having anything to do. I very very seldom bring any work home and I do not stay one minute after four o'clock. I get all the work done in school hours. The timetable works fairly well but I don't think a half hour is long enough for arithmetic so I make it longer. The school was freshly painted and is very clean now . . . I took the kids out to play ball this afternoon . . . They are not very good players but it was a bit of fun . . . [During her six-week training course at the Winnipeg Normal School Hazel's Phys. Ed. class consisted of "how to play softball."] . . . I enjoy listening to the radio sometimes. When I haven't got much to do I wish that there was more entertainment. I guess that I can't have both nothing to do and enjoyment as well.

Hazel's loneliness increased and on September 15 she wrote:

Dr. Clingham from Virden came and vaccinated and inoculated the kids for diphtheria today. Some of the kids under school age were brought. There were about a dozen there I guess . . . We went into Elkhorn on Saturday night. The dance was not much good . . . However . . . it helped to pass the time. On Sunday we went to church . . . situated away out in the bush. No music to sing the hymns by. What a primitive way of living or I guess you would call it existing . . . Gee how I wish I was in Miniota . . . Sometimes we get a ride home from school. If it rains a bit in the morning Mr. B. generally takes us to school. I wish it would rain a little every morning and then clear up . . . If you hear of any way I can get home phone me, eh? I guess I can stand it this weekend, but I would like to get home the next one.

Ten days later, on September 25, Hazel's frustration was clear:

Gee, I'm glad this week is almost over. It has been really miserable hasn't it? I got back here on Sunday night about 10:30. They were all in bed but it didn't make any difference to me . . . Remember on Sunday we were experimenting with the alarm clock? When I was going to bed Sunday night I thought that it would be a good idea to set the alarm as I was tired. I set it and it rang at two o'clock and nearly scared me out of my wits. It is the first time that I ever set an alarm and now I know how. Always learning something eh? . . . I started out on Monday morning and made all the kids learn the Lord's Prayer. Of course it was just a small job as I have so few. Tuesday was about the wettest day yet wasn't it? Coming home (walking of course) it rained and hailed . . . Remember I told you that the stove smoked a lot? [Like many young teachers, when Hazel began at her school she had no idea how to light a fire.] Well on Tuesday after we got the fire going (and what a job) it smoked such a lot that we had to go outside. We just had to do without a fire, that was all there was to it. I told Mr. B. about it and he said he guessed that they would have to try to fix it. I felt like saying fix it or find another teacher . . . Wednesday morning . . . he phoned up a fellow who lived near the school. He went over and fixed it a bit but it still smokes. When I got to school there were only three kids there. However I started in just the same as if there were twenty which I wish there were. At noon hour the inspector came. He is rather a nice man. I told him about the small attendance, but he said nothing could be done about it. When he said that I almost felt like telling him where to go . . . He only stayed a little while. Asked me a few questions about the work and looked at some of the scribblers. When he was going he told me he thought I was doing good work, especially in arithmetic. At the rate I am going, when he comes back again the grade fours will be about in grade six. That certainly was a long day. Just three kids to teach, and that is only the beginning. Yesterday when I went to school only two turned up . . . I waited until about ten o'clock and then I told them to go home and came home myself. The

dickens with teaching two kids. I don't care whether the
school board liked it or not . . . Anyway, I earned my pay by
walking to school and back in the cold. It is four miles alto-
gether . . . When I got to school today low and behold there
was no one there . . . This is beginning to get past a joke . . .
So I had two holidays with pay that I didn't expect. Some
holidays, though. Not a single thing to do. I heard the Happy
Gang both days so that was something. They played "You'll
Get Used to It" today. Guess I will some time. [The Happy
Gang was a popular radio program in the 1940s and 1950s.]

Hazel hung in.

October 3—I don't think that I will write home this week. You
can phone Mum and tell her that I'm fine . . . tell her that I
will phone her on Thursday night . . . Also ask her what I am
to say about Marian coming here. I would not like to men-
tion it from this end of the conversation as there are many
ears wide open . . . Sometime you will have to tell the
Miniota kids that I am wondering how they are getting
along. Tell Eddy that I am still living, I think . . . They are
threshing here today so there is a little more excitement.
There are about ten men . . . We are going to take out the
lunch this afternoon. Then I guess that we might have some
fun . . . Mr. B. got word that he was to take ten dollars off
my cheque for Normal. That means that I won't need to pay
any income tax. The tax amounts to about ten dollars so it
is about the same in the end. If I didn't have to pay it for
Normal I'd have to pay it in taxes.

But Hazel simply couldn't overcome the feelings of isolation, frustration and loneliness that threatened to consume her. By mid-October she knew she would not stay.

October 17—The days are slipping by slow, but sure . . . I have not seen anyone nor had a bit of mail all week . . . I had a good trip back here. As good as could be expected, of course, considering the place I was coming to and the driver . . . I was talking to Irene the other night . . . She is leaving at Christmas too. Gee, I'll be glad when that day comes . . . One day on the way to school we saw a pheasant, a weasel, and a badger hole right in the middle of the road. Talk about the wilderness. This place has them all beaten. We hear some of the queerest noises sometimes. I have had about the same number of kids. They just seem to come whenever they feel like it. What difference does it make anyway—the less I say and think about school the better, I guess. If I ever get away from here I'll never want to look at another school again . . . I haven't taken any more pictures yet. There does not seem to be anything worth taking. Next time I'm home (Halloween, I hope) I'm going to leave the camera with Buffy. Then there'll be something worth taking.

Just when things seemed their worst a starburst of happiness put the glitter back into Hazel's eyes. It flashed briefly, lighting up her skies before fizzling out into the dark once more.

October 23—I had quite a bit of fun last weekend . . . We went to the dance and Bobbie and Lloyd were there. I had lunch with Bobbie . . . We happened to get talking about shooting so that was just fine. I finally got Bobbie persuaded to go out shooting on Sunday or I mean he got me persuaded to go. We went out on Sunday afternoon about a quarter to three. Just had a twenty-two and two boxes of shells, but we had lots of fun. We shot mostly at tin cans and bottles . . . I guess I'm not a bad shot because we would line the bottles . . . up in a row. Bobbie would tell me which one to shoot at and where to hit it and I could do it almost every time. Of course he wasn't bad himself . . . We went into the school and fooled around. He was quite interested in the composition that some of the kids wrote . . . I got paid last night. $50.53. By the time that they take off the ten dollars for Normal and $2.80 for retirement fund it hardly pays to bother with the rest . . . All good things have to come to an end so Bobbie phoned me up today at school . . . He said that he was going home this afternoon so that was that. He hated it in this country as much as I do. Just came out here for harvesting . . . It is so cold in the school and the stove smokes worse than _ _ _ _. Fill in the blanks. I tell them about it but it doesn't do any good. They are going to get a surprise around Christmas time, I'm telling you . . . Did you listen to Treasure Trail this week? B's think that it is too late. Late I'll be D _ _ _ _. Fill in the blanks once more. When school starts at 10:30 we certainly are going to get some sleep. I am so sick of sleeping. I was tired last Sunday night for about the first time since I came here. That was after we had walked a good many miles in the wilderness.

Hazel did indeed make it home for Halloween, only to face several shocks when she returned.

November 5—I got back here safely as you have probably guessed by now . . . I went to bed but hadn't been asleep very long when I woke up and felt sick. I had an awful stomach ache and felt dizzy. After a while I vomited all over the floor (at least over part of it). Then I don't think I slept any more till morning. I felt rather bad (in more than one way) in the morning so I didn't get up. Finally Frances [a student] came up to see what was the matter and I told her that I was sick. Thank goodness I vomited or I wouldn't have had any proof. That was one day that I didn't have to teach . . . I felt alright on Tuesday so started off once again. When I got to school someone (not the school kids for they were as surprised as I was) had been doing Halloween tricks. The school doesn't lock so people just walk in and out whenever they like. Guess it is handy when anyone wants to use the phone. [Not locking the building in case someone needed it was a common practice in many rural schools.] There have been several people in the district complaining about someone on the [phone] line that the school is on. They think that it is the school kids. It isn't though. If anyone needs to complain it is me . . . When I walked into that school this is what had happened. I will just list some things that I can think of: desks twisted around; pegs, letter tickets and number tickets spilt all over the floor; an oat sheaf broken up on the floor; brooms in the attic; old decorations brought down from the attic; mercury and HCl acid spilt; stove pipes bent in; windows cracked; the bell taken apart; a box of pen nibs spilt on the floor; a gramophone record broken; two blinds torn off the rollers; one blind had been used to wipe up some dirty water; the door was wired shut from the inside with about one and a half feet of barbed wire, (they pounded a nail into the wall to hold the wire); one of the windows was open wide; the flag was fastened to the stovepipes. They wrote all over the boards. One thing was "This is Halloween—Miss Green." I felt like adding some to it . . . The boys' toilet was almost wrecked and the girls' was full of sheaves . . . It is a big wonder that you didn't see me home again . . . I haven't had any mail or any parcels this week. Guess that they would be in town if I could only get them . . . I phoned Irene but she didn't know anything very exciting. There was such a noise on the line . . . Irene and I stopped and listened. It was interesting. Shux, Mrs. S. hasn't got a thing to complain about. She should be on one of these lines. I guess that is the only way people here get news. [A reference to people listening in on telephone party lines.]

On November 14 Hazel once again had something exciting to write home about.

I went into the Young People's Rally last weekend. It was very nice and I enjoyed myself. Last Friday night we went to a shower and dance at Kola (a school near here). They had a whist drive and I won the ladies prize (a war savings stamp). Imagine my surprise!!! Everyone looked at me when I went up to get it. Guess they wondered where in the dickens I landed from. After the dance I went to Miss Brown's place (the Kola teacher) then on Saturday morning she and I went into the Rally. We came back on Sunday afternoon with the minister. We had to listen to speakers for a while and then we were free. It was very interesting . . . On Saturday night we went to the dance. There was a big crowd there and I had about the best time I've had yet. School starts now at 10:30 and ends at five o'clock . . . I went into a concert and dance on Wednesday night. I was certainly glad that school started at 10:30 on Thursday . . . The dance didn't end until after three o'clock. How did I go? Wouldn't you like to know? I went in with a Corporal who is home on leave. He lives near here. I met him on Saturday night at the dance. He is home for two weeks . . . it isn't very long till Xmas now thank goodness. I've had about all that I can stand. Poor attendance. Oh, gee it isn't worth wasting ink over. M.B. was home for two days. She is stationed in Winnipeg now. The lucky so and so. Every time I hear of anyone going to Winnipeg I feel like taking the first train myself.

Finally the end was in sight. On December 2 Hazel wrote:

I have finished giving the kids their exams. I made out the reports tonight. Now for concert work and then the end. So far the word has not got around. At least I have not heard anything. Buffy saw me post the letter [of resignation] so that is all I can do. I posted it in Elkhorn. Of course some people don't get their mail very often. There is a big surprise waiting for several people. I don't know what they'll say when they find out but who cares? I'm sure I don't . . . Talk about cold weather. I have been wearing my ski suit to school. I've kept my ski pants on all day. It was so cold . . . There were quite a few planes flying over when we were going to school. That sort of broke the monotony of walking in the cold and frosty wilderness . . . The news is on now so I guess it will be bedtime for all very shortly . . . I might have to write in the dark if I don't hurry.

But one more tribulation awaited Hazel!

December 5—We are busy practicing for the concert at school

now. School still closes on the eighteenth as far as I've heard . . . Oh gee the bubble broke the other night (Friday). It started after I came home from school. Frances came home and said that the reason I was leaving was because I didn't like the boarding place. Of course they immediately approached me on the subject and I denied it. I have never mentioned not liking it. The kids at school started it. I am going to have a terrible time, I'm afraid, but thank goodness we are near the end. I guess I'll have to wrap up the presents when they come. That will help to break the monotony of it all. Guess I can write bigger now that no one is trying to read this . . . I feel awful about that rumour. They said that I just stayed here until I couldn't stand it any longer then I had to go home. Who wouldn't want to go home once in a while even if they did like it? . . . If you see some poor broken down old thing coming down the road it will likely be me.

At last it was over. In her final letter home on December 12 Hazel wrote:

They had a school meeting last night at the school. I was present and at it they accepted my resignation. I will be home on Friday. I guess about all I'll have to do that day is clean up the school . . . I got the presents for the kids. They were mostly the same as what I sent for . . . I just heard "Santa Claus is Coming to Town." That is the song Marie is singing at the concert. We are getting along fairly well with the practicing . . . Things have quietened down now and everything is OK Very nice in fact. Too nice. I hate that.

Even though Hazel only lasted one term as a six-week permit

teacher she is a survivor. She had the good sense to get out before she was turned off of teaching for good. One wonders how many there were who would have made good teachers but were deterred because they tried too young with too little training.

Hazel worked at odd jobs until she finally decided to return to teaching. This time she went to university, earned two degrees and only then began a long and successful career in the profession.

"But in the beginning it was too rough," she openly admits. "I just couldn't handle it."

Mary

. . . .
. . . .

 In 1940 Mary Werklund was living in a lean-to on the side of her husband's garage in Valleyview, Alberta. They were a young couple full of dreams, one of which was to farm. The teaching shortage precipitated by war came at a good time for Mary. She had been a teacher since 1930 but, as was expected of women during the Great Depression, she had left her position when she married Paul in 1937. Now her skills were again in demand, just at a time when Paul was ready to sell the garage and buy a farm. Mary's income as a teacher would go a long way towards helping make ends meet on the two quarters they purchased just east of Valleyview.

Mary and Paul were spirited and determined. When Mary was hired to take charge of a school many miles from their new home they were undaunted.

"We had no car," she remembers. "Our only vehicle was a rubber-tired wagon and a team of horses over very poor roads. We went south to the Ridge Valley School, then turned west to go down and up the steep-steep banks of Cornwall Creek. Then south again to a road allowance, then west a few miles to the school. There was no place for me to stay so Paul built a small cabin in the schoolyard and here I stayed through that term."

It wasn't easy. They had a two-year-old son to think about.

With careful planning they managed to give Donnie the time he needed with each of them. Paul often made the long trip out to spend a weekend. Sometimes he took Donnie back to the farm with him, and other times he left the tyke with Mary.

Mary was an experienced teacher and slipped easily into her former role. She taught fourteen students, grades one to eight, in the Simonette School and enjoyed a happy, productive year. Only one incident blemished her time there.

"It was the war years," she relates. "People were fearful. Also, people were very very hard up so farmers shot rabbits to raise a few extra dollars. They carried their guns always in their sleighs with them. One weekend we held a dance at the school. All came in the sleighs. Some boys found a gun in one outfit and shot it off."

It was fairly harmless fun for the boys and Mary thought no more of the incident until the following week when the inspector arrived at her schoolhouse door. He said nothing as he meticulously searched the school. Mary watched and wondered. Finally coming up empty handed the inspector questioned Mary about the shooting. He was visibly relieved when she explained what had happened at the dance. Apparently she had been reported for allowing guns in school!

A successful year over Paul came in June in a covered wagon to pack up Mary's things and take her home.

"Off we headed on a two-day trek through mud and water," she says, "with a small sun-tanned boy looking out the back. As we drove past Sturgeon Lake we met Indians on horseback. They followed behind us peering at that small blond, brown-brown boy and no doubt wondered who their new neighbours were."

Mary didn't return to Simonette School in September. She was too busy with farm life and, after December, a newborn daughter. The following year, when Linda was eight months old and Donnie was four, she took on her biggest teaching challenge yet—forty-two students in eight grades at a school just three and a half miles from home.

The Calais School was a draughty log structure with a homemade wood-burning oildrum heater that was barely sufficient for the job. Despite the devotion of the twelve-year-old twins who came one and a half miles each morning to light the fire before the others arrived, the school was still freezing. Mary conducted classes facing the backs of the students as they huddled around the stove.

"With forty pupils, some had to sit on the outside," she remembers, "and they were as cold as I was in my snowsuit and boots . . . while those on the inside were overcome with heat."

It turned out to be one of the coldest winters on record. Mary drove a one-horse cutter (closed-in sleigh), picking up as many children as she could along the way. Others walked, rode, or drove their own outfits. Some had up to six miles to travel.

The temperatures didn't stop any of them. The boys especially could hardly wait for recesses and noon hours to get outside and pursue their passion for hockey. No skates, no equipment and no ice were minor drawbacks.

"A stick from the nearby bush was a hockey stick," says Mary. "The rink was the snow or bare ground, and frozen horse manure their pucks."

With ten grade one students, "very little blackboard space and little equipment," Mary had her hands full. She often asked the older pupils to help the beginners when their own work was done. One beginner, Norman Adolphson, called the grade five student who helped his class his "teacher." Her name was also Mary. She mustn't have done any harm, for at the time of this writing Norman was the mayor of Valleyview!

During the long cold winter at Calais Mary launched a special project to help the children occupy their spare time indoors.

"I made Mickey Mouse quilt blocks for them to embroider," she says.

The children took pride in stitching their own individual square, carefully embroidering their initials on the work, but when spring came the blocks were forgotten in favour of softball and other outdoor joys.

"My teaching career for the forties ended that year at the end of June," says Mary. She didn't return to the classroom until twelve years later, when her youngest son Stephen entered school. In 1964 she retired for good.

What became of the quilt blocks? Twenty-eight years after retirement, eighty-one-year-old Mary tracked down former students still in the area and together they finished the quilt. It hangs in the school division office and when not there is on display at various public venues. It's a community treasure!

Hilda

Nobody was more surprised than Hilda Nelson the day secretary-treasurer H. K. Fielding of Hanna, Alberta and Fred Rossler of the Bingo District, appeared in the Chinese restaurant in Coronation. They had an offer for the young waitress who had just graduated from the Coronation High School, class of '44. Would she supervise correspondence lessons at Bingo School, southwest of that town?

Hilda was completely taken aback. She said she'd have to think about it and went home that night to consult her parents. They were enthusiastic. Hilda was the only child of a family of ten who finished high school. She knew her father wanted her to become a teacher. Ever afterwards she wondered if he'd had a hand in the visit to the restaurant that day.

At the end of the summer Hilda's brother Emil helped her get established in the teacherage. Once he was gone Hilda felt lost. It was a new experience living alone and she wasn't sure she liked it. She was used to a bustling family environment with lots of people around.

The first day of school was nerve wracking. Hilda didn't know any of the children and wasn't sure how they'd like her. She did know that she would start the day with Bible reading and the Lord's Prayer. She was greatly relieved to discover that the students' correspondence lessons were all in order and ready for them to proceed.

It didn't take long for tensions to ease as Hilda and the children got to know one another. She had eleven students. It was like exchanging one family for another.

"Within a week Inspector Aikenhead from Hanna was out," she relates. She was further relieved to find that he was "very pleasant and helpful."

Things were off to a good start!

Hilda kept a meticulous school register and was also responsible for janitor work. She swept the floor after school each day and cleaned the blackboards and brushes. She chopped wood and kept the pot-bellied stove well fed.

"The children were always willing helpers if needed at any time," she warmly recalls.

Hilda was good to the children too. She took pleasure in organizing "little parties on special days" like Halloween, Christmas and Valentine's Day. Games and related amusements were enjoyed with delectable treats to follow up. She often invited the parents too.

"Noon hour and recesses were something to look forward to," she adds, "playing games such as hopscotch, softball . . . hangman, and hide and seek . . ."

Fox and Geese was a popular game played outdoors in the winter. A large wheel with a pattern of spokes radiating from its centre was tramped into the snow. One student, the fox, stood in the centre. The others, the geese, distributed themselves around the perimeter. The fox commenced to chase the geese. The resulting flurry was akin to a coyote in a chicken coop, except that in trying to avoid Mr. Fox the geese could not step off any of the beaten paths. Neither could the fox. As soon as one goose was caught he or she became "It", the fox became a goose, and the game began again. The children spent many, many hours at this lively passtime.

When they arrived at school in the winter the students set their lunches beside the stove to keep them from freezing before noon.

"They also often brought potatoes and put them on top of the stove," remembers Hilda. "With that smell it was hard to wait for lunchtime."

Hilda's first paycheque was $48.05, not much more than some teachers paid for room and board.

"The children paid for their own supplies," she recalls. "Scribblers [were] two to seven and a half cents for Jumbo size, crayons seven and a half to ten cents, pencils three for five cents, erasers two for five cents, rulers three cents, manila drawing paper ten sheets for one cent."

School days were pleasant, but at her teacherage Hilda battled boredom. The evenings were long with little to do. She was grateful to have a radio to provide at least the illusion of company. Her two brothers in the army benefited from the time she had on her hands. She filled up many hours writing letters to them. She also took a typing course by correspondence from the Garbutt Business College in Calgary.

"When possible on weekends some of my family came down," she says. "It was good to receive some of Mother's canned fruits, vegetables, pork and beans, etc."

Often Hilda's younger sister Ellen stayed with her for a while. Not only was she good company, she was a willing pair of hands as well.

"She helped paint the interior of the teacherage [and] together with a neighbour helped lay linoleum."

Hilda's neighbours were extremely good to the young supervisor living away from home. The Rosslers were right across the road and the Saars one mile away. Both families offered her smiling welcomes any time and she enjoyed many meals and evening entertainments with them, skating, impromptu concerts, playing games or just visiting.

"The little hamlet of Spondin some miles away had two grocery stores, post office, creamery, elevator and hall," she remembers. "Saturdays I went with either the Rosslers or Saars to do my mailing and buy groceries."

Once in a while Hilda got the urge to call home. Then she walked to the Lehman farm to use the barbed-wire phone.

"This was run on the fence line. As long as the wire didn't break from cattle or heavy hoar frost it worked [well]. Later other residents had them until government telephone service became available."

The following year a teacher was found for Bingo School so Hilda didn't return. By this time she had married her "sweetheart and best friend," Ben Adolf, and had moved with him to their farm near Spondin. She had proven her worth to the school division, however, and her services were still sought. The Gooseberry Lake School was only two miles away and in need of a supervisor.

Here Hilda had nine students and once again she was nervous, "not really knowing any students or parents." Her fears were unfounded. They liked her and she liked them. Off to a good start again!

Hilda sometimes drove to school in their Chevrolet coupe. This wasn't always practical. Roads then were neither paved nor gravelled. When conditions were wet or snowy, Ben took her by car or sleigh. More often than not she walked.

Fortunately, a fellow who lived near the school was hired to do the janitor work, for no longer did Hilda have time on her hands. What she calls "the regular farm life" took up all of it: "cleaning up the garden . . . canning fruits and vegetables . . . a cow to milk morning and night . . . the tub and washboard to do laundry."

Occasionally the teacher from Bingo School stopped in for a meal, keeping Hilda up to date on all her former charges.

In January a teacher was also found for the Gooseberry Lake School. Hilda was happy to have time to devote just to Ben and the farm.

Her freedom was short-lived. By September Bingo School was again without a teacher. They put in a special request for her and she agreed to return. She was all set to begin at the start of the school year when misfortune struck. Both she and Ben contracted yellow jaundice on the same day. There was no way Hilda could start school in that condition. She asked special permission to commence school a month late, on October 1st. The school board generously agreed.

"It was good to be back with the same children," she recalls.

But roads were no better getting to Bingo than they had been getting to Gooseberry Lake. When it rained there was real danger of getting stuck in the mud, which Hilda did several times. When the snow came Ben drove her the two and a half miles with a team of horses and a sleigh. Even that proved difficult as it turned out to be an excessively cold and snowy winter. In November they decided that Hilda should live in the teacherage for the coming months.

It was a wise decision for more than just Hilda and Ben. Mr. and Mrs. Rossler were expecting another baby. The hospital was miles away in Castor. As a precaution it was important to get

Mrs. Rossler there several days before the baby was due. They set out in early January, leaving their oldest girl to look after the rest of the family. It was a comfort to know that Hilda was right across the road! She was already grateful for the many kindnesses the Rosslers had shown her and was delighted to have the chance to pay them back. She did everything she could to help the family in their mother's absence. She made meals, baked bread and buns, and even caught them up on some mending. During the evenings they passed the time by playing games. On January 9th a baby boy was born.

"There was excitement in the family when mother and baby arrived home."

Before long the winter was over and Hilda moved back to the farm.

"Back to muddy roads again," she sighs. The mire was so thick that when she drove the car to school she needed chains on her tires. Spring's advance eventually dried the roads but until then they were often all but impassable. In the meantime Hilda had to get to school. Imagine what the neighbours thought as she trundled past them perched on the farm's Ford tractor!

Despite mud and snow, cold temperatures and boredom, Hilda's two and a half years as a supervisor were rewarding. She would've made a good teacher, but this was the closest she ever came to the profession. The farm and raising a family of her own came first and was, ultimately, every bit as rewarding!

Diana

In 1945 Diana Phelan (now Rae) was eight years old. Eventually she would go to Normal School and become a teacher, but for now she was a shy, quiet grade three student in a country school near Selkirk, Manitoba. She'd had a wonderful teacher the year before, a minister's wife whose daughter, the same age as Diana, had been a good friend. But the minister and his family had moved away and in the blink of an eye Diana lost both her favourite teacher and her favourite friend.

Now her school was assigned a permit teacher, a sixteen-year-old girl not from the area. Sixteen-year-olds were big people to Diana and she knew she must always obey her elders. It wasn't until years later that she realized what a terrible mistake the trustees of her school had made.

Diana's little sister was in grade one that year and, as the oldest, Diana was put in charge of her safekeeping. She took the responsibility seriously. Each morning the pair set out walking to school, eventually meeting up with the neighbours who gave them a ride by horseback the rest of the way. Each afternoon Diana saw her sister safely home in the same manner. It wasn't long before she realized, however, that ensuring her sister's safety and well-being was going to be much harder than she imagined.

The new permit teacher was a nightmare. She had a deeply disturbing sense of humour. Diana never knew what was coming next—or when.

"She did the darndest things for fun," Diana remembers. "She used to pretend she was a ghost sometimes at recess. She'd dress up and try to scare us."

Diana knew better than to believe she was seeing a ghost, but her little sister was terrified.

The janitor of the school was one of the older students, a boy about twelve years old. He was quite lax with his duties, often not bothering with them at all. One day the permit teacher decided she'd had enough. She would fix him! She ordered all the students to help her make a mess of the school. They did everything they could think of to cause chaos, even tearing up papers and throwing them into the air to cascade down over everything. Diana sensed that something was wrong with this 'assignment', but what choice did she have?

"We just did as we were told," she shrugs helplessly.

Of course the plan backfired. The boy simply refused to clean it up. He hadn't bothered with his regular chores. Why should he bother with this?

"We ended up having to clean up all this mess [ourselves]."

As far as Diana could tell, nobody else seemed concerned about the odd antics of the strange teacher.

"I went home and told but nobody really worried about it. I think maybe they thought it was just something they had to put up with. Maybe they were just so afraid of losing the teacher."

Diana resigned herself to a difficult year.

Then came the day the eight-year-old was shocked down to her very toes. With a devilish grin the permit teacher announced that she was going to throw Diana's sister into the fire! She grabbed the girl and dragged her to the stove. What a jolly time she was having!

Diana stood petrified and frozen to the spot. Part of her knew that the teacher was bluffing.

"I kept saying to myself, 'She wouldn't really put her in. I know she wouldn't really put her in.' But what if she got too close to that fire? What if she got burned? I was supposed to protect my younger sister. It scared the wits right out of me!"

Her sister survived the joke, but from that day forward Diana was doubly on edge. She had always been timid, now her nerves were frayed to shreds.

At the end of June the school closed and the following year the children were bussed to Selkirk. Diana looked forward to starting grade four in a new school with a new teacher. But another shock was in store. When they arrived in Selkirk they learned that almost every one of them had to repeat the previous year's grade.

"I think there was one older kid who didn't," says Diana. "They just explained that we hadn't covered the work at all. We were deprived of a year's education, more or less."

Diana was devastated. It bothered her tremendously that she had failed.

"I was a good student. Well, once I repeated grade three I was a good student. They put me in the advanced reading class in Selkirk, but the other subjects I had to do all over again."

As the years went by Diana put the experience behind her. Her child's mind rationalized that she had obviously over-reacted since her parents hadn't been unduly bothered. When she grew older and trained to become a teacher herself, however, it dawned on her how wrong the situation had been.

"I knew so many young girls who had been permit teachers

and I knew they would never have acted like that," she says. "*I would never do anything like that. Even at sixteen I know I wouldn't have.* This is what troubles me. How [these girls] could get into teaching. Besides academic qualifications there should've been something else. But I guess nobody checked. They were so short of teachers, I guess they just took whoever they could get."

War

· ·
· · · · · · · · · · · · · · · ·

 Maxine Sutherland was an experienced teacher. By the time war broke out in 1939 she'd been in the field for eleven years. She'd come through the destitution and dust of the depression. Now she faced new challenges.

"Suddenly school and community projects lost meaning," she laments in her memoir *From Desk to Desk in Canada, 1914-1974.* "Dread and helplessness was the feeling of those days . . . Gradually as the war became a day to day fact, school and community began to matter again, but however pleasant the school and community activities were, there was always that terrible backdrop of war."

One of the most sinister aspects was the suspicion and hatred engendered for the "enemy." Many German and Italian immigrants populated the prairies. They and their families were immediately labelled enemy aliens even, in some cases, if they were naturalized citizens. Japanese-Canadians too were regarded with malice. In years since, apologies have been made, but during and immediately after the war, emotions ran high and many regrettable actions took place.

One of the first things that occurred was the government's registration of all residents of Canada. Teachers and school boards were solicited to help. Catherine (Elm) Linden-Jones, (Claudia's sister), remembers helping her mother register people at the local school. Every person had to produce proof of Canadian citizenship and give his or her father's racial origin. For example, her father had come from the United States, but had to declare his Swedish origin.

Lillian Coulson, who taught at Orangeville School near Sangudo, Alberta, remembers being "ordered to fill in a booklet on each family."

"The school inspector came around and assisted in this," she says. "It required the origin of every family. These were given to the secretary of the school division. After the war I asked the gentleman what finally became of them. He said, 'After the war I took them all out back and burned them in the trash can.'"

An atmosphere of mistrust was ever present. People of German, Italian or Japanese descent were 'watched' and had to report regularly to the RCMP. Firearms were taken away and in some cases not returned, even after the war.

"Families from Germany formed a little group and stayed away from the rest of us," says Lillian. This propensity probably contributed to the damaging rumours which were quick to spread. Walden Smith, who taught at Sunnybrook School near Warburg, Alberta remembers that one resident was accused of harbouring the German flag in her bedroom. Others claimed Germans had hidden away powerful radios that they used to send 'spy' messages back to Germany.

In schools, opening exercises included saluting the Union Jack while reciting the Pledge of Allegiance:

> *I salute the flag, the emblem of my country*
> *Red is for courage; white is for purity; blue is for loyalty*
> *I will be brave; I will be pure; I will be true*
> *God save the King.*

For whatever reason some students refused to do this. It wasn't legally required, but to refuse at a time when loyalty to one's country was uppermost on everyone's mind cast the offender in a very bad light, often with negative consequences. One boy in Warburg was made so uncomfortable he found it necessary to transfer to Sunnybrook.

"I don't care. Let him come," said Walden. "I didn't worry. We had to salute the flag every morning but I turned my back and saluted it too. So if half the kids didn't salute that was their business."

Walden was a peacemaker. When fights broke out in the schoolyard he was quick to intervene.

"We're all one blood," he told his pupils. It saddened him when two of his most vehemently anti-German students could hardly wait to become old enough to join up. They both hurried off to war—only to be killed in action.

Maxine was another teacher who displayed compassion and tolerance. When she heard of a school near Rocky Mountain House, Alberta that couldn't find a teacher for its predominantly German population she asked for a leave of absence from her own school to help out.

"There was said to have been trouble over the display of the Canadian flag and the Union Jack," says Maxine in her memoir. "Some of the pupils were supposed to have refused to speak English."

Evergreen School turned out to be a very rewarding experience, due in large part to Maxine's sensitivity and respect for all people.

"The first week of school there were one or two pupils who spoke a bit of German now and then," she relates. "I ignored this. We were all soon very busy and interested in school activities."

Maxine had a penchant for music and theatre and used this to bring about a profoundly healing experience.

"We prepared a program of songs and dances and invited the parents and friends to come to the school. We made a back-drop . . . of the flags of all the nations liberally mixed with Union Jacks and Canadian flags. In our folk-song presentation we included the Lorelei. Spontaneously the adults joined in, some of them singing in German . . . I've always thought that the singing of the Lorelei that afternoon in Evergreen School released much tension. After all, the Evergreen people had come to Canada long before the rise of Hitler. Their community raised more money for the Red Cross war effort than many others in Alberta at that time. At Friday night dances as much as $300 would be handed over to the authorities who were usually present in the person of the RCMP . . . Some thought the raising of money for the Red Cross was just 'a show of loyalty'. I never believed that . . . When I left Evergreen School at Christmas I was sorry to leave the peo-ple, the school and the pupils."

Later in the war Maxine taught at a school near Taber where many coastal Japanese-Canadians were evacuated to work in the sugar-beet fields. One very bright Japanese boy enrolled in her school.

"He was plainly . . . apprehensive," she recalls. "I felt much sympathy for him. Any trouble which might have developed was prevented by my presence on the playground at recess and noon hours. I saw to it that the boy was included in all the games, but no one made friends with him."

The boy's mother was so grateful to Maxine for her kindness that before the family was relocated yet again she presented Maxine with a gift, "one of those colourful and handy little sewing kits with needles, threads and pins."

"I was deeply touched," says Maxine. "As these people had been taken out of their homes almost without notice, they'd had little time to gather possessions. That Japanese lady perhaps needed that sewing basket more than I."

Registration with the authorities entitled people to ration booklets, perhaps the most tangible evidence that things were not as they used to be. The federal Wartime Prices and Trade Board placed price controls and rationing on innumerable consumer goods because they, or the materials from which they were made, were in high demand for the war.

New cars and farm machinery couldn't be had. If new tires were needed they were made of sub-standard synthetic rubber. Gasoline was rationed to 120 gallons of orange per car per year. Purple gas was not rationed but was restricted to farm machinery only. The RCMP randomly monitored road vehicles for its use. Some creative consumers got around this by filtering the purple out through a loaf of bread.

Nylon stockings had first appeared in 1939 but were not yet common and silk was needed for parachutes and the like, so leg paint became popular. Available in several shades, the trick was to apply it evenly to bare legs with a small flat brush. A touch of authenticity was sought by drawing a thin seam up the backs of the legs with an eyebrow pencil. According to Hazel (Green) Smith, these fake stockings were "great, if it didn't rain!"

One case of beer and one bottle of hard liquor per month could be obtained with a liquor permit card. Ration booklets allowed each family a quota on such things as coffee, tea, sugar, butter and meat. Walden Smith recalls, "You got so many coupons [redeemable at the store] and when those were gone you went without."

That was the way it was supposed to be, but not necessarily

the way it was. A spirit of cooperation prevailed as people pulled together to help each other. Walden kept bees and sometimes traded honey for sugar. Lillian's neighbour, a European immigrant, gave her his extra gas coupons.

"He was a bachelor," she explains, "and seldom went anywhere but town." Besides, he was "always willing to give a helping hand if needed."

Ethel Howes, whose story appears later, was raising a family when rationing took effect.

"When my husband picked a pillowcase of saskatoons I needed to can them without sugar," she recalls. "Because we had ration books for each of the children who did not consume their full allowance we were not in need for ourselves . . . we [also] bought a cow, chickens, pigs. Having [our] own helped supply our needs."

Many teachers who boarded were encouraged to turn over their ration coupons to their landlady. When Mabel (Wheeler) Hobbs attended the Moose Jaw Normal School in the summer of 1947 she and her classmates were advised not to relinquish all of their coupons to their summer landladies. The women at the places they'd be boarding when they went out to schools needed some as well. Where Mabel eventually boarded shortage of meat was never a problem because the men hunted deer. However, "Meatless Monday" was a practice that the public at large was urged to observe.

To aid with the war major recycling projects were launched years before they became an environmental issue. Here again schools were recruited to help. Ruby (Plomp) Anderson recalls the children collecting salvage.

"Several commodities were needed for war-related industries," she observes. "We collected clean rags, lard, grease, aluminum and dried animal bones. These items were weighed, boxed and stored in the porch until a truck arrived to take them to a depot in town."

During the depression of the thirties many animals had perished on the drought-ridden prairies. Lack of feed for cattle and horses meant slow death for some and instant death for others. Mabel remembers with anguish her father taking out and shooting their two oldest horses because they couldn't be fed. Other animals perished in blizzards and storms. Their bones on the prairies were a goldmine for explosives manufacturing. They also went into making glue and fertilizer. Fertilizer was needed to grow vegetables vital for feeding the troops.

Collected rags were used, among other things, for making gun wadding, haversacks, and seat padding for tanks. Scrap metal and iron were collected too. They were also plentiful on the prairies in the aftermath of the depression, when thousands of farms and their machinery were abandoned. Even the little things mattered: tin foil from cigarette packages and metal toothpaste tubes. In the drive for used rubber for things like tank tires, dinghies and oxygen masks, even worn out clothing elastic was sought. One former student remembers a tiny pair of rubber boots on the schoolhouse shelf amongst the other items gathered. And Leonard Wold remembers his father donating a large pile of old rubber tires.

Students were avid participants in work for the war effort. Walden Smith's Sunnybrook School had a "War Workers Club."

"They put on different bazaars," he says, "or sold pancakes or cakes and things like that [to raise money] for the war effort."

For twenty-five cents each the children bought war stamps. When Mabel was a high school student in the two-room Carmichael School in Saskatchewan they held competitions to see which class could buy the most.

"When you had five dollars you had what they called a certificate," she explains. "You sent them to Ottawa, they were processed [into bonds] and after so many years you could cash them out."

Mabel earned money for her war stamps by moving cattle for a neighbour.

Junior Red Cross Clubs were also active. The Red Cross supplied cotton and wool, along with instructions, and boys and girls alike learned to knit facecloths, socks, vests, and afghan squares. They hosted dances, box socials and other events to raise money. They also wrote letters to service personnel, many wondering in years since what kind of reactions their childish encouragements induced.

Teachers too were active in their respective communities. Ladies' Aid Societies and Women's Institutes flourished across the country. Ruby remembers being invited to join the one at Kingsley.

"Many of the projects were aimed at helping in some way with the war effort," she says. "Ditty bags were sent to the Merchant Marines or one of the other armed forces. Boxes of goodies were sent to local boys and loved ones, some stationed in Canada and some overseas. We sent letters as well and . . . proudly read aloud answers we had received. The Red Cross supplied wool for mitts, scarves and socks. All of us knitted squares to be sewn together for warm afghans . . . The ladies set up quilts in various homes. They gathered for "quilting bees." They sold tickets on these lovely items or raffled them off, with all the proceeds going to the Red Cross or some worthy war effort. Money-raising concerts were planned and held in local halls or nearby towns."

Freda (Daymon) Longman was representative of many teachers.

"Even though my salary [of $900 per year] seems small by today's standards," she relates, "I was able to purchase several war savings bonds to help in the war effort!"

Sadly, it was while she was teaching and too far away to return home that she learned of her brother's death overseas.

During the war many teachers found it difficult to teach Social Studies (a new subject consisting of History and Geography combined). The world scene was constantly changing. Others took advantage of the situation.

"Following the progress of war by studying the world map on the wall," explains Ruby, "helped the children learn history in an interesting, relevant way."

Other schools had the luxury of a radio and listened to the School News Broadcast to keep abreast of current events. In the evening what became known as Lorne Green's "Voice of Doom" kept most people glued to their radio sets for the nightly newscast.

On 'Victory in Europe' (VE) Day, 8 May 1945, there was heavy celebrating in the streets of cities and towns across the country. Rural communities gathered together and if a band could be found they danced out their joy until dawn.

Within weeks veterans began arriving home. School boards and provincial Departments of Education everywhere were certain that the teaching crisis was over.

To everybody's surprise and dismay it wasn't. Many former teachers didn't care to return to the low wages and substandard living and working conditions they'd endured before they left to broaden their horizons at war. Additionally, incentives to veterans for service to their country encouraged many to attend university or pursue training in other fields at government expence. The teaching shortage was not alleviated. If anything it grew worse.

Laura

. . . .
. . . .

Because of the continuing crisis after the war, Laura McMurray supervised correspondence lessons in a country school for two years before a teacher was finally found to take over. She had wanted to go into nursing but crops were poor when she graduated from high school in 1946.

"Money wasn't to be found for me to further my education," she recalls. "When Mr. Stan Hambly came to the farm and offered me the chance to supervise . . . I was overjoyed!"

Kirkwall School, southwest of Oyen, Alberta was approximately fifteen miles from Laura's home. While there she lived in a one-room teacherage exchanging rent for janitor work in the school. The inevitable loneliness suffered by so many in her situation was eased by a unique companion. An amiable old tomcat came around and decided Laura would make a worthy cohort. He moved right in.

"The teacherage was heated with a coal and wood cookstove with an oven," she says. "This cat would be back in the oven in the morning to keep warm."

Laura also had the unheard of luxury of getting her groceries delivered right to her door.

"I was lucky to be on the mail route which ran from a country store at Excel," she relates. All she had to do was walk up to her neighbour's and call in her order from their phone. The mailman brought it out along with the mail!

Laura enjoyed supervising and had little trouble, perhaps in part because she was quick to catch on to the children's high jinx. The very first day they queried with artful innocence as to whether she was afraid of mice.

"I quickly answered, 'No, I like mice'," Laura winks. "So I never found any in my desk!"

Another time one of her grade one students refused to do his work. Laura was unperturbed. There was nothing going on at the teacherage anyway.

"I can stay as long as you can," she told the boy, and so they did, long after the others had gone home.

While she waited for the youngster to change his attitude Laura busied herself with chores, one of which required leaving the room to get coal for the stove. She didn't know until years later when the culprit told her himself that every time she left he "put a stick in the stove and then stuck it in a hole in the wall trying to burn down the school."

Back in those days getting into trouble at school usually meant trouble at home as well. At nightfall the boy's mother came looking for him and quickly took him in hand. He didn't come to school the next day but showed up the day after that, having obviously decided that doing his lessons at school was preferable to being made to stay in bed all day.

In truth Laura felt sorry for the grade one students struggling to learn by correspondence. If the work that was sent in at the end of the month "wasn't perfect, the whole scribbler had to be repeated, plus the next month's work [done] as well."

Laura provided some fun for her students when she could.

"On cold winter days when the weather was nasty," she says,

"we filled snuff boxes with sand, made rings on the floor and pretended we were curling at recess."

The Booker Heater was a force to contend with. Anyone daring to check it by peeping in was treated to a burst of flame, often having his or her hair singed for good measure.

"It burned slack coal which produced lots of ashes," remembers Laura. "Once the ash pile caught on fire so I had to fight fire and watch all night that it didn't start up again."

In the two years Laura was at Kirkwall she definitely earned her pay: four dollars a day the first year and $4.85 the second. Once she contracted jaundice and another time came down with red measles!

In June of year one she was gratified that all of her students passed their grades. In May of the second year a freshly graduated Normal student was sent out to replace her.

"The school division offered to put me through for a teacher," she says, "but by then I wanted to get married."

Laura married Ken Carr in July of 1948 and together they raised a large family of their own. She remembers her time as a supervisor being "a rewarding experience." Certainly good practice for her subsequent eleven children and twenty-seven grandchildren!

Ralph

Ralph Derdall was a member of the Royal Canadian Army Medical Corps Reserve for almost two years before he graduated from high school in Outlook, Saskatchewan in 1945. He had planned on moving into active service but the end of the war on May 8 changed all that. Suddenly Ralph had to choose a different direction for his life.

"During the summer holidays a brochure arrived in the mail," he recalls, "with information and pictures about the Normal Schools in Saskatoon and Moose Jaw. They looked very interesting. I talked it over with my parents and they thought it could be good to carry on with my education. As the deadline was fast approaching I hurried to fill out the application and send it off."

On 19 August 1946, almost exactly a year later, he began his first job in a one-room country school.

Cherry Dale School was five miles west of Strongfield, Saskatchewan.

"It was an exciting experience to have my very own students ranging from grade one to grade ten. My salary was $1000 for the year."

What wasn't so exciting was the teacherage beside the school. Like Laura, the rent Ralph had to pay was cancelled in exchange for doing the janitor work in the school.

"The first snowfall came October 3," he remembers, "which was the beginning of a fierce winter. My teacherage had no insulation and no storm windows. When the temperature dropped to thirty-five degrees below zero on the Fahrenheit scale accompanied by strong winds, it was virtually impossible to keep warm."

After building the hottest fire he could, Ralph set up a rotisserie arrangement with two chairs in front of his stove.

"I would . . . sit on a chair with my feet on another chair facing the heater to get warm but then my back would be freezing so I'd turn around to warm my back, then back again to facing the heater. After soaking up some heat I would run up to the school to keep the fires going there and back again to my 'rotisserie'."

Unfortunately, he couldn't sleep in those two chairs, and eventually had to make a dash for the bed.

"Crawling out from under a pile of blankets in the morning was invigorating to say the least," he recalls. "The ice in the basin and water pail had to be thawed before I could wash and shave."

Ralph enjoyed teaching his dozen-plus students. He had several first-generation German, Polish, Czechoslovakian and Norwegian children. There were no tensions; everybody got along well. Ralph particularly enjoyed helping the students stage a Christmas concert. He couldn't read a single musical note, but clearly that was no obstacle. A natural ear had scored him the highest in Normal School for musical ability. The highlight of his first concert was an operetta based on the fairytale Rumplestiltskin. He also had a number of students performing with tonettes, a basic type of recorder.

"I had my little tonette band playing in three-part harmony and it sounded rather nice," he smiles.

Rehearsals for the concert took priority as the all-important date drew near.

"Nobody felt deprived by skipping our regular classes," he chuckles. "Rehearsals were fun and in their own way educational."

The night of the big event the schoolroom glowed, the "hissing of the gas mantle lamps and the crackling of the fire" creating a warm, intimate mood. The evening was a resounding success, made even more special by the obvious appreciation Ralph's students and their parents felt for him. He came away loaded with gifts and kind words.

After the excitement of Christmas the cold winter dragged on. Roads were so snow-choked that operating motorized vehicles was out of the question. The only way of travelling was by walking or horsepower. For sanity's sake it was imperative not to be cut off from the world. Despite the cold Ralph regularly made the ten-mile round trip by cutter to curl in Strongfield.

When the snow finally melted, swampy, mucky mires still prevented the use of vehicles. It wasn't until late spring that Ralph received his first visit from the school superintendent.

R.J. Penny was sufficiently impressed that he offered Ralph a new position for the following year: the teaching principalship of the two-room Birsay School, which was "in need of a disciplinarian."

Ralph was surprised and not at all sure he was the man for the job, but who was he to turn down the school superintendent?

"26 August 1947 I [was] back in the classroom," he states, "facing a class . . . from grade seven to grade twelve. I was only nineteen years old . . . teaching students nearly my own age. One returned air force veteran enrolled in grade twelve and was four years older than me. I wondered what I had let myself in for."

All across the country war veterans returned to multi-graded country classrooms. Were it not so common it might have been awkward. As it stood, it was simply a sign of the times.

Walden Smith of Sunnybrook School says that it was no different teaching the veterans than it was the other students. He does recall one fellow approaching him with concerns about being treated like a child. "Don't you give me hell," he said. "Don't be hard on me." And Walden replied, "Don't you worry. I'll never give you hell about anything. You just come back and there'll be no problem."

And there wasn't. Veterans who returned to school were there for a purpose and completely committed to their education. They worked hard and many advanced to university.

"They were star students," says Walden.

Of his returning student, Ralph states, "I hardly knew he was in the room because he worked so diligently."

Strangely, their experiences at war were never spoken of. Aside from the difficulty of discussing such things in a multi-graded setting, there was simply no opportunity for it in the curriculum. Ralph goes one step further when he says, "There seemed to be no need for it."

Despite his earlier trepidations Ralph had a good year at Birsay. He and Patricia Steele, the grade one to six teacher, made a good team. It was just as well because Ralph was allotted no 'spares' to perform his administrative duties as principal.

"It was quite a juggling act to teach, give assignments, move from one class to another and keep everyone busy."

Again the winter was long and harsh with impassable roads. At Christmas Ralph commuted to his home in Outlook and back by train and sleigh with little difficulty, but he wasn't so lucky returning to Birsay after the Easter break. It took four days to travel less than thirty miles.

First of all, the Outlook Dray (delivery horse and cart) took him to Denny's Siding, a boxcar beside the tracks down which the CN train for Birsay came. Ralph recalls the horses "jumping" through the snow on the highway because it was too deep to walk. When he got to the boxcar he "started a fire in the heater to keep warm while waiting for the passenger train."

"By sundown," he says, "the train still hadn't arrived, I'd burned up all the wood so I had no heat and no lights." Ralph had no way to flag down the train in the dark.

"Finally a freight train came by slowly. I had no choice but to grab my bag and make a run for it and managed to scramble onto the caboose."

He didn't make it far. At Macrorie, less than halfway to Birsay, the train ground to a halt in the deep snow. The passengers were stranded for the night while crews worked to free the train. The next day they resumed their slow journey only to get stuck again at Dunblane, just a few miles from Birsay. This time they were delayed two days "while work crews [shovelled] snow by hand to clear the tracks."

It seems odd to struggle so hard to get back to a place where you know you'll be confined in isolation for the rest of the term.

"The spring thaw was a most welcome sight," remembers Ralph.

In June he decided to take a leave of absence from teaching and, as it turned out, a full ten years went by before he was in the classroom again. By then things had definitely changed. Country schools were rapidly vanishing as centralization took over. The war had brought the world into the classroom and boundaries were stretching to accommodate it. Field trips, previously frowned upon or forbidden, were commonly accepted. Civics was stressed. Audio-visual equipment, expanded libraries and other resources were more and more prevalent.

"I'll never forget how great it was to get back to the chalk and blackboard and students," Ralph remembers.

He retired in 1985, and of his first two years' teaching he concludes, "I . . . gained experiences . . . teaching in the forties that present-day teachers will never have."

Mabel

. . . .

. . . .

Because Mabel Wheeler (now Hobbs) had a good average in grade eleven at Carmichael School in Saskatchewan, before she finished grade twelve her principal was urging her to enroll in Normal School. What Mabel really wanted was to be an architect. Her high school teacher had even searched out information for her about it.

"The only architecture school was out in Vancouver," she relates. "I knew Mom and Dad couldn't afford to send me."

So Mabel decided to go to Normal School. In 1947 the Moose Jaw Normal School ran an eight-week summer program designed to place Normalites in schools by September. They were then to attend eight-week summer sessions for three years to complete their certificates.

Mabel's Normal School instructors were a diverse lot. Many were district superintendents teaching through their summer holidays. Others were regular Normal School teachers who stayed on for the summer. The principal too stayed all year round.

"He didn't seem to take holidays," observes Mabel.

She took about thirteen different subjects, including instruction in deportment that she never forgot.

"Our drama teacher put us through how we were to stand

up on a platform, and how we were supposed to sit and walk and all that kind of stuff."

All the students were tested for proficiency in the English language and some (primarily those who didn't speak English at home) had to take special remedial classes.

There were no summer holidays for Mabel that year or the three years following. The first Tuesday after Labour Day she opened classes at the Kealey Springs School twenty-two miles south of Piapot, Saskatchewan in the Eastend School Unit. This suited Mabel perfectly. She was a farm girl who did not take well to urbanity when her father moved them closer to town during the war for her high school years.

"The first school I took I wanted to be as far away from town as I could get," she declares, "and I wanted to ride horse-back to school."

Mabel had ample opportunity to enjoy country life while she taught. From her $100-a-month paycheque she paid twenty-five dollars room and board to a farm family.

"If they wanted to go to town on a Saturday night I would stay in and milk their cows or milk them Sunday morning if they stayed overnight."

This was nothing for Mabel. Ever since age fourteen she'd done men's work on the farm, due in part to the manpower shortage during the war.

"When the men weren't there to thrash the teenagers took over and did it," she relates. "I used to haul grain to the elevator with a team, and shovel grain back from the thrashing machine and off into the bins with the old grain scoops."

It didn't bother Mabel not to get to town much, even for Christmas shopping. After all there were Simpsons and Eatons mail order catalogues for everything a person might need. She did feel the odd agonizing twinge of loneliness though.

"Once we left home," she says of herself and others like her, "we never got in touch [with friends and family] except by letter. You couldn't phone home or anything. We didn't have phones where we were. We were just expected to grow up."

Mabel did manage to get home for her sister's wedding in the fall.

"They were having a dental clinic in Piapot so I went into Piapot, caught the train and went to Carmichael. It was about thirty miles."

At Christmas Mabel got home the same way, which turned out to be a happy circumstance for her.

"In those years we had to balance that register at the end of each term," she bemoans. "I had no idea how to balance it, but I'd met a teacher who was teaching at a school east of me and she got on the train at Piapot too."

Together, between Piapot and Carmichael, they worked out Mabel's register. Mabel was forever grateful for the kindness of the more experienced mentor.

As far as her own teaching went, Mabel discovered the advantage of having so recently been a student herself. The course of studies was still fresh in her mind. She had about a dozen students from grades one to nine. Because there were so few, grades three and four, five and six, and seven and eight were grouped. For example, one year the grade three and four class were given the grade three curriculum and the next the grade four curriculum. It was hard on the younger ones who went into grade four work first and then took grade three the following year, but Mabel asserts "you couldn't teach them all, you just couldn't get around, so you had to group."

In those years it was common for parents to send mentally

challenged children to school. Their disabilities were largely downplayed or ignored. Mabel had one such child.

"I don't think that I did very much for that little girl," she says with genuine regret. "We didn't have any training in how to teach them or give them reduced classes or anything like that. And there certainly weren't many supplies in the school. You had a baseball and a bat, a basin and a water jug and some old maps maybe, and not much for a library."

Mabel did have one big advantage over other teachers. Her uncle had recently visited from the states and brought her his old typewriter! She hated the hectograph, a messy, time-consuming way of copying exams and seatwork. Master copies were written out with a special purple pencil, then laid face down onto the dampened hectograph (French gelatin melted into a cookie sheet and cooled). The writing transferred to the jelly. By smoothing additional sheets over it, one at a time, extra copies of the work were made. In the process, wet purple ink soaked into hands and everything else. The hectograph had to be scrubbed if it was needed again soon. Otherwise it was left overnight while the purple writing soaked into oblivion.

With the typewriter, Mabel avoided the whole messy business.

"The largest class I had was four students," she recalls. With carbon paper it was easy to produce up to four copies of a typed assignment. An extra advantage was the ability to design "matching" and "fill-in-the-blank" questions. With so many grades, blackboard space was limited and assignments placed there had to be mostly essay-type.

Mabel also had another useful teaching tool.

"I scrounged around and got a radio and then I bought the A and B batteries you had to hook them up with. At that time they had a school program on every afternoon for about half an hour. There wasn't an aerial outside but if I tied [the radio] to the metal cream can the kids got water in it came in nice and clear."

Occasionally "institutes" were held, akin to today's professional development days for teachers. Mabel recalls that these were "always Saturdays. Never school days taken off." One Saturday Mabel caught a ride into Eastend to attend an institute on a new exercise for Physical Education.

"I took my own money and bought a couple of mattresses advertised in the *Western Producer*. They were war surplus cot mattresses and they came by mail. In those days everything came by mail."

Mabel's pupils were good athletes. They won the Shield that year for track and field—a coveted prize. It was a salve for her shortfall in teaching music.

"I don't think my [Christmas] concert was very great because I'm not a singer. We didn't have any piano or organ in the school. We had a fellow come over with a violin and play the music for us."

Mabel still made a good impression on the district. The year after she left Kealey Springs School they wanted her back. She may have made a better impression on them than she did on the school superintendent.

Like many women teachers, Mabel was in the habit of wearing slacks to school then changing in the outhouse.

"You couldn't wear slacks in school," she explains. "You had to wear a dress."

One morning she swung open the outhouse door and was surprised by an equally startled skunk.

"He didn't spray me," she says with relief, "but he got the skunk smell on my pants."

After changing, Mabel hardly thought twice about hanging her slacks on the fence to air out during the day. Of course that was the day the superintendent arrived unannounced. There were her pants, "blowing in the wind," and there was Mabel, red-faced before a disapproving superior.

This wasn't Mabel's first contact with the man. He'd been one of her instructors at Normal School, so she was already aware that he was rather humourless. On that first visit to her school he was equally disapproving of the way she kept her register.

"He got out there and he drilled me," she remembers, "and I guess I was a good learner because I certainly caught on." In later years Mabel was praised for the consistently excellent condition of her registers.

One thing in particular brought comfort to Mabel's and the children's day. Each morning they filled a large enamel kettle with water or snow and set it on the Waterbury stove. Food brought in jars was placed in the kettle and by noon had simmered into a satisfying meal. Warm tummies helped make sharp minds.

In June Mabel left Kealey Springs School to return to Normal for another summer of study. Before she did, however, an unfortunate incident took place.

"Somebody stole the two mattresses and took my radio. The district knew pretty well who had done it but the couple had gone to work in Alberta. Everyone figured they'd just stopped off at the school and packed up the stuff."

Shades of Frances Ost and her stolen box of books!

Fewer students returned to Normal School that summer.

"Some had gotten married," recalls Mabel. "Some just didn't want to pursue teaching any further. They'd had too rough a time maybe."

By the third summer the class was smaller yet. According to

Mabel this was partly due to the opposition teachers with only a few weeks of training faced from others in the field.

Mabel persevered, taking courses for many summers, even after she had children of her own. She learned that if she was careful to first make sure they applied to her certificate she could accelerate her training by taking some courses in Alberta, where twice the amount of work could be accomplished in one summer.

"I went to Calgary and took the four kids for three weeks and stayed with my sisters. Then they went home and stayed with their Dad while I finished."

Mabel made good use of all her training. Even though she retired a full twenty years ago she has continued to serve as a substitute teacher. The last few years she has filled in on a near full-time basis as a teacher at the Okimaw Ohci Healing Lodge, a correctional facility for Aboriginal women outside Maple Creek, Saskatchewan.

Many years have passed since a nineteen-year-old dreamt of studying architecture. Many students over those years are no doubt glad she didn't!

Caroline

"Truly I don't know which is the schoolteacher," remarked the elderly lady as she watched children play ball at Glen Elmo School in 1945.

The package was indeed deceptive. Five-foot-tall, ninety-five pound, seventeen-year-old Caroline Parobeck (now Antoniw) was accustomed to heavy farm work. She was not intimidated by tall schoolboys who disobeyed or by the prospect of using the strap.

In fact, it was while milking cows in the barn that Caroline had her first encounter with the school inspector. The silhouette in the doorway wanted to know if she was interested in teaching in a country school thirty miles from her home near Angusville, Manitoba.

Caroline couldn't believe her ears. "I had just completed grade eleven," she says, "and was anxiously waiting to continue my grade twelve. Ever since I was in grade four my heart's desire was to train for a schoolteacher . . . There were no funds for going to higher education, which entailed money for books, room and board, etc. I was the sixth child from a family of twelve children so my chances . . . were even slimmer. But I studied hard and entreated my father to allow me to continue my studies."

There was no need for that. Suddenly a teaching job fell right into her lap.

"Without any preparation I ventured into a classroom of thirty-six students, grades one to eight plus two correspondence students."

Caroline wasn't letting this chance slip by. She worked hard, determined to do a good job.

"I went . . . two hours before school and put work on the blackboards, wrote out little lessons for grade one and two pupils, etc. . . . I worked late into the night to correct work and prepare . . . for the next day."

She already knew how to use a hectograph. She had often helped her own teacher copy seatwork and mark assignments in the elementary rural school she had attended. Now it was Caroline's very own students helping her.

"My grade seven and eight students volunteered to help me correct the lower grades' arithmetic and spelling books while we ate our lunch. Then they said, 'Miss Parobeck, please come and play ball with us.' I usually went . . . and we became like one happy family."

Which is not to say Caroline didn't encounter problems. Like Joyce from South Head School she seemed to have an instinct for handling them. One boy crossed the line three times one day and was ordered to stay after school. When the fatal hour arrived Caroline still wasn't sure what she would say.

"As I was debating what my opening words should be," she recalls, "he began to cry. And I said, 'How would you like to be my helper?' Then I told him all the work that needed to be done. I needed someone to bang some big nails for hanging clothes in the porch. The blinds needed some fixing and several other jobs needed to be done."

It worked like magic. The boy was only too glad to turn destructive energy into constructive behaviour. Another time

Caroline found it necessary to strap a student. She did it "in front of the class."

"After that," she says, "I didn't have to use the strap. In those days when the strap was in the school, discipline was not a problem."

The janitor work was shared by all.

"The teacher and students raked the yard in the spring," she remembers. "We washed windows and polished them with crumpled newspaper. The students took turns sweeping floors and cleaning blackboards."

In turn, Caroline helped at her boarding house. Like Mabel, when she couldn't get home weekends she helped with threshing and milking cows.

"I was quite an outdoor person," she relates, "and I enjoyed helping . . . to get away from books for a while."

The school was only an eighth of a mile away but it wasn't always easy to get there. All Caroline had to do was walk a path, traverse a bridge and cross a road, but at times the snowbanks were so soft and deep she couldn't get through them. Innovation was needed.

"I threw my lunch pail and my school bag over the bank and rolled over [it] in my fur coat."

Caroline's salary was sixty dollars a month. Even though she paid nineteen dollars room and board, it was a windfall for the girl who had all but lost hope of being able to afford further education. Now her dreams of becoming a 'real' teacher were in sight.

But there were obstacles. She returned to school the following year to take grade twelve and soon discovered it wasn't easy.

"I didn't do so well in my chemistry because I had forgotten some of my grade eleven work. Before that I had never failed any subjects at school. I wrote two supplements in August. These were to be corrected at the Department of Education in Winnipeg."

In September Caroline moved to Winnipeg and prepared to attend Normal School. On the first day she stood in line to register with beating heart. Her dream was finally coming true! As she reached the front of the line she was stopped short. Where was her letter of acceptance, the registration clerk wanted to know, and what about the marks for the supplementary subjects?

"I didn't know I had to have a letter," says Caroline. "Neither did I receive my marks. I was told to go to the Department of Education and inquire . . . Can you imagine? Caroline—a green cucumber from the country! I had never been to a city, didn't ever ride a streetcar let alone find my way to the correct department at the Legislative Building."

Caroline suffered a few moments of serious doubt. Perhaps she should just get on the train and go back home.

But no!

"I was determined that . . . I would take my training and become a teacher. I did find my way and I sat on that chair and said that I'd wait till my papers were corrected and I'd get my letter of acceptance."

Clearly it was the right decision.

"I enjoyed all my years of teaching," she says, "and still wish I was at school."

Now in her seventies, Caroline continues her professional calling.

"I teach adults with upgrading lessons [and] I also teach Ukrainian lessons to English adults. Once a schoolteacher—always a teacher!"

Dorothy

Dorothy (McDonald) Linklater still has the zippered black case her proud father gave her when she graduated from Saskatoon Normal School in 1943. It was "to make me look like an 'experienced teacher' for my first day," she warmly recalls.

In a way, Dorothy was already experienced. While at Normal she had filled in several times as a substitute teacher in another school. The first time there was no advance notice. She was simply approached by the Normal School principal one morning and told they needed a substitute immediately at St. Mary's School. She was even given streetcar fare to get there!

"It was quite a challenge to walk into a room of grade seven pupils without any preparation," she states. "They were very cooperative. I don't think they realized I was only eighteen years old."

The fact that Normal School operated in another school that year because the air force had taken over the regular building was also a bonus.

"The Wilson [School] students being in the same building . . . proved to be very advantageous for me to hone my skills as a teacher . . .doing remedial work in Mathematics and Spelling, one on one, with students who were having problems. I found this a very rewarding experience, encountering practical accomplishments and knowledge which I would not have had in Normal classes."

Upon graduation at Easter Dorothy was delighted to be assigned grades five, six, seven, and eight in the three-room Coleville School. Coleville was perfectly situated, halfway between Kerrobert and Kindersley.

"This was very convenient for me to catch the CNR train at Kindersley to go to Zealandia in the summer when my dad farmed, or the CPR train from Kerrobert to Sovereign where he owned the Town Dray in the winter."

Dorothy kept things lively and interesting for her twenty-five students. She taught them to square dance and held tap dancing lessons for the girls after school.

"One day there was a carpenter at school and I knew he was a square dance caller," she reminisces, "so we invited him in to call for us. It was 'Dip and Dive and Outside Under' that he taught us to dance and sing. What fun!"

Each day after lunch the students loved to listen to Dorothy read from a good book. On wintry Friday afternoons they walked to the outdoor rink to skate from recess until home time.

The students especially enjoyed singing and never missed an opportunity to put words to song.

"Our Christmas concerts were always musicals," she observes. "My favourite . . . was a Minstrel Show, 'Won't You Come Home Bill Bailey'. This included everyone to sing and two boys to be End Men. When a matriarch and a young mother heard about it they offered to make two zoot suits for the boys, with baggy pant legs, narrow cuffs and broad lapels in brightly coloured plaid. The boys had a pocket-book in a pant pocket and a chain hanging from it. These two boys were . . . natural comedians. They didn't have TV to see such things then. The laughter was very timely and loud. Above everyone you could hear the jolliest and tiniest grandmother in the hall."

Laughter was needed, for like most towns and districts in those years, Coleville was blighted by the dreaded polio. Poliomyelitis, also known as infantile paralysis, is an infectious viral disease that prefers to target children and young adults. During the forties no vaccine had yet been developed and epidemics were rampant, killing many and leaving many more with varying degrees of paralysis. Because it tended to strike in August and September, school boards often delayed school openings for a month or so. Youth gatherings were discouraged and in some areas forbidden.

But young people weren't the only ones affected. It was a good ten years after Dorothy left Coleville that a successful vaccine was finally put into use. By then many more, including adults, had fallen to the disease. When Dorothy returned for a reunion fifty years later she "found it very sad to hear [of] many young mothers and fathers [who had passed] away and [left] young children behind."

Dorothy left Coleville in June of 1945 to teach a grade five class in the city of Saskatoon. Again she had twenty-five students but found the job much easier without the pressures of multigrades and extra tasks in a rural school.

She taught there one year before marrying in 1946. It was a year she'll never forget.

"My most vivid day there was very emotional," she recalls. "There were three brothers in the school and the middle one was in my class. Their mother was dying of cancer and their father was a prisoner of war in Hong Kong. It was often discussed at recess in the teachers' meeting room as to how these boys were coping. Stress was not a common word then so we never approached them. One morning there was a knock on my classroom door, which usually meant the principal or the superintendent—but there stood a very tall man. [He] looked like a skeleton. Immediately I realized it was the father and he asked if I would excuse his son for the day."

Dorothy was extremely grateful that the rest of the class didn't see the cadaver-like figure. She was certain it would've been too horrifying. This was the first person she herself had seen come home from the war. The devastating reality of the last six years hit her with stunning impact.

"I was very shaken. It was as though I had been crying for hours, as it left me with an occasional sob and wiping a tear from my eyes . . . The class remained very subdued and understanding . . . We had celebrated the end of the war at Coleville on 8 May 1945 with lots of red, white and blue streamers. But this bleak fall day in Saskatoon was not for celebration."

Muriel

On a dark winter night in 1945, up against temperatures exceeding minus twenty degrees Fahrenheit, seventeen-year-old Muriel Berry and her fifteen-year-old sister Leone set out walking from the teacherage of the Valley Plain School twelve miles north of Quill Lake, Saskatchwan. They had no choice. There was no phone, no nearby neighbour, and they wouldn't make it through the night with no fuel for the fire. The trustee who had forgotten to deliver their wood lived three miles away. The strong wind and deep snowdrifts made it seem like thirty. They pushed on.

It was just one more challenge of the many Muriel had faced to fulfill her dream of becoming a teacher. She was one determined girl. Against all odds (including a father who didn't believe in higher education), she pursued her heart's desire. After finishing grade eight at the Quill Lake View School near her family's grain farm, she enrolled for three years of high school in Clair, the nearest village.

"I drove back and forth the seven miles each day by horse and buggy in summer," she says, "and by horse and cutter in winter."

Grade twelve presented an even greater hurdle. The nearest place to take it was Wadena, roughly twenty miles away. That meant moving there and boarding for the year. How could she possibly afford that? Despite questioning her ambitions, her father came through for her—but she had to earn it.

"[He made] an agreement with me that if I helped take off the crop in the fall of 1944 he would pay for my grade twelve in Wadena and a course in Normal School in Saskatoon. So with tractor and combine I harvested the grain crop in time to enrol for grade twelve in Wadena."

When she graduated the following spring Muriel needed special permission to attend Normal School, for she was only sixteen years old. She got it.

Saskatoon ran a six-week summer program that year and in September, for $1,000 a year, Muriel began teaching in the Valley Plain School. She had just turned seventeen.

Dotted throughout the lake regions of Saskatchewan are thousands of crude cabins, thrown together often with nothing more than odds and ends and intended simply as holiday havens in the summer sunshine. It was in one of these uninsulated shacks, hauled to the school grounds from a nearby lake, that Muriel and Leone lived—in exchange for cleaning the barn, the outhouses, and the school.

"In the winter the nail-heads on the walls were frost-covered and if the bed was too close to the wall the blankets were frozen to the wall. The water in the tea kettle sitting on the stove was frozen in the mornings."

The school was also cold, and so draughty that on winter mornings after lighting the fire Muriel turned to the task of "sweep[ing] snow from the windowsills!"

"The stove was . . . a barrel on its side that used the long cordwood and these would have to be dug out of a snowdrift."

The stovepipe was strung along the ceiling to help spread warmth through the room. Stovepipes were put together in segments that had a nasty habit of occasionally coming apart and clattering to the floor. In the process they showered soot and dust all over desks, books, floor and people. Fixing them required climbing to reattach the hot sections of pipe. Then of course everything had to be cleaned. Magdalene's stovepipes in the old school teacherage at Wanham fell down three times. Muriel's only fell once, but that was quite enough.

"Thank goodness for tall boys to help get [them] back together," she observes.

Muriel's "tall boys" were five students who were almost the same age as she. Her strategy for avoiding discipline problems was to treat them as peers. It worked beautifully, but she discovered the drawbacks of the approach when she was "criticized for socializing with students more than parents at gatherings."

"But of course I was closer to them in age," she explains.

Muriel's grade nine and ten students studied by correspondence. She still provided assistance and developed and marked exams for them. She regretted that with so many grades she couldn't spend more time with each student. One little scholar was so keen to learn that he took matters into his own hands. He finished one reading assignment then plowed ahead to the next and so on in his grade one reader. Muriel suspected he was merely memorizing so she asked him one day to start at the end of the lines and read backwards. He happily complied. He was so pleased with himself that he took the book home to read to his mother. He returned the next day beaming.

"I can read it all and backwards too!" he announced to the astonished Muriel.

Muriel was also baffled by the way in which three small sisters travelled home after school. She often helped them hitch their horse to the cutter on cold days.

"They would jump in the cutter, pull a blanket over their heads and give the horse free rein," says Muriel. "The horse would be cold from standing all day in an uninsulated barn and, wanting to get home, would take off in a gallop. I was always amazed that the cutter did not tip over as it rounded the curve going out of the schoolyard!"

As Christmas concert time approached Muriel felt excitement mixed with apprehension.

"In those days," she remarks, "I think the teacher was judged more by the concert she put on than by how well she could teach."

There was no way of making music in the school. Muriel managed to borrow an organ and then found a friend to play it. She was less lucky with her Father Christmas.

"The first year the Santa chosen was a shy man and didn't utter a single word and not one 'Ho-Ho'."

Somehow they made it through. Muriel and Leone's parents even came to watch the concert before taking the two girls home for Christmas.

The annual concert wasn't the only social event Muriel was responsible for.

"The school was well known for its whist parties and dances," she recalls. "I was to soon learn that it was up to the teacher to organize and plan them, to make the lunch and hire the orchestra."

A formidable task for Muriel had never even played cards let alone organized whist parties. It was a great advantage that she got along well with her students. They were happy to show her the ropes and even helped coordinate the entertainment.

The Field Day in Quill Lake was another event in which Valley Plain School had a reputation for excellence, "especially in the parade marching." It fell to Muriel to maintain the standard.

"Each spring we spent considerable time practicing the different events and the marching."

Spring was also the time for playing ball. It was exciting to have nearby schools come to compete, but reciprocating depended upon Muriel being able to "find a parent who was willing to drive [the] team to a neighbouring school."

"At those times I would be called on to be the umpire," she remembers.

In the winter of 1945-46 excitement ran high as veterans returned home from the war. One such soldier was Lewis Nicholls, the older brother of one of Muriel's students. A romance between Lewis and Muriel soon developed and blossomed, even after Lewis left for Sudbury, Ontario to work in the nickel mines.

Muriel went back to Saskatoon Normal School the summer after her first year of teaching, then returned to Valley Plain for another year before joining Lewis in Sudbury to get married.

Today she has five grandchildren, some of whom are in university or college, following their grandmother's example by pursuing their own higher educations.

Ethel

. . . .

. . . .

When their farm on the prairie near Hawarden, Saskatchewan was hailed out in August 1940, Ethel and Fred Howes relocated to Saskatoon. Fred found war work in a machine plant and Ethel busied herself with their growing family. While there they traded, sight unseen, six work horses from their farm for a quarter section of land in the bush country near Hazel Dell, Saskatchewan. In July of 1942 they journeyed up to the unfamiliar territory to view their new home.

A log cabin on the site needed renovating. Other than that it wasn't too bad. Milk cows, chickens, pigs, turkeys and ducks would do nicely here. Moreover, the Woodrock School nearby had been without a teacher for some time. Ethel hadn't taught since her marriage in 1936 but she was ready and willing to get back into the profession that she loved.

While they renovated the cabin, Ethel, Fred and their three daughters— four, two and just a few months old—lived in the "granary-like, eight-by-ten-foot teacherage" near the school.

"It contained a table, two chairs, a wood stove and a pull-out couch," comments Ethel. "The floor was bare floorboards . . . [There were] a few essential dishes, pots and pans enough for one . . . water for drinking and cooking . . . brought from the school. There was a slough . . . nearby . . . for washing, [and] bedding enough for the one pull-out couch."

Fortunately, their log cabin was ready four weeks later, even though it meant a swampy, half-hour walk through the woods for Ethel to get to school. One day she had to drop a fallen tree over a racing mass of water and manoeuvre over it trapeze-style to get to the other side.

"It was risky," she states, "but compared to walking across open spaces with bullets flying intended for live animals in shooting season [it was] mediocre."

Once the family was settled into the cabin something strange occurred. They began receiving unusual numbers of visitors. People were generally neighbourly but this was beyond reason. Ethel had hired a neighbour to be her baby-sitter. She finally asked the girl to enlighten her as to why they were blessed with so much company.

"She explained that it was to see the teacher's home," says Ethel.

By this time their belongings from the city had been delivered and people were fascinated by the sophistication of all the modern things.

"Many had never seen such—only in magazines. They had, in many cases, very primitive, homemade furniture."

Ethel had fifty students from grade one to eight. She was less daunted by the numbers than by the names, most of which were Ukrainian and difficult to pronounce. Before long they established rapport and were busy at work. Ethel was amazed by how well-behaved the children were.

"They were so happy to be in school with a teacher [that] they aimed to please," she smiles.

When haying time approached some of the students came

to Ethel and reluctantly told her they'd have to stay home to baby-sit toddlers while their mothers went out into the fields. They would much prefer to be in school. At one student's tentative suggestion Ethel agreed to let the youngsters come to school.

"If they are as good as you are," she told them.

"Next Monday I had not the usual fifty, but seventy-five. They shared their seats, scissors, crayons, mucilage, etc. They could not have been better."

The tots took turns sitting with their various brothers and sisters in school and Ethel was extremely pleased that "classes went on as usual. No interruptions."

The majority of the children spoke Ukrainian at home, but speaking anything other than English at school was forbidden. For the most part the children were good about this rule but when they got excited it was easy to slip into their mother tongue. This happened one day while they were decorating the school for Christmas. Ethel couldn't follow the conversation, and although she had no objection to the language, wondered if she should stop them because it was against regulations. Before she could decide they apparently speculated as to whether she could understand them.

"Someone asked me if I knew what 'peh-te-boy-yah' was," she says. "It was the only word I knew. I casually answered 'potatoes'. That was all that was needed. Someone [said], 'See, she does know.' There was no more talking in Ukrainian!"

There were no such regulations outside of school, however. Some months later at a picnic Ethel encountered her baby-sitter and several students speaking to her one-and-a-half-year-old in Ukrainian. She was stunned to hear her daughter answering in the same language.

"She had learnt [Ukrainian] before learning English," marvels Ethel.

It was customary for many rural schools to break for several weeks in mid-winter due to weather and road conditions, then make up the time in the summer months. Woodrock School was one of these, closing for six weeks after Christmas. The timing was good, for Ethel was exhausted. Leaving her husband to look after the farm she packed up her three children and took the train home to Glenside to visit her parents.

"It was a jolly time," she recalls. "The girls were well cared for by my mother as I replenished [their] wardrobe by dismantling three coats and making them a winter outfit apiece . . . as well as many other things."

Ethel also helped her father do books in his office, a job she had enjoyed when she lived at home years earlier.

"All seemed well until the children came down with the measles and I discovered I was pregnant," she says. "Would we be able to travel home in time for the opening of school? We were, but on the train I discovered evidence of chicken pox."

This was not good, according to the school board. Ethel was requested to stay away from school until her children had recovered. Even though she produced literature stating that she couldn't spread the disease, it was feared the school children would be harmed. Whether she wanted it or not, Ethel's winter holiday was extended.

"Perhaps this rest helped my condition," she reflects.

Ethel did believe in rest. She was in the habit of setting aside half an hour each day after lunch to read to the students.

"I let them know that if they so desired they could rest their heads on their arms, close their eyes, and if it so happened that they fell asleep that was all right."

One day while reading Ethel suddenly folded to the floor in a faint. The horrified children were certain she was dead. They fled en masse from the schoolroom to the farm across the road to report their teacher's untimely demise.

"It was at this point," laughs Ethel, "[that] I awakened, found myself lying on the floor and my pupils vanished . . . Then as I looked out the windows I saw them trooping back, headed by the lady from the farmhouse . . . They were surprised I was alive. I insisted on carrying on classes for the afternoon. My short rest had revived me. The lady insisted on staying. She walked home with me after school."

As much as Ethel had surprised the students, they were about to surprise her. The annual sports day in Hazel Dell was coming due.

"When I announced it," she recalls, "I got the reply that they never took part. They had always considered that day as a holiday [and] stayed home and worked."

Ethel was flabbergasted.

"First of all I made campaign speeches about the value of such an event," she says. "To them and their parents it was a wasted day with no returns. Eventually they were enthused after we made a huge banner of cloth with appliquéd letters of the name of our school district, supported with two tree limbs to hold it aloft as we marched."

But there was still opposition. Many claimed no one would show up. Ethel was adamant.

"Go or not, we would practice."

Her hard work was ill-rewarded. While some did attend the sports day with eleven other schools in Hazel Dell (in fact, Woodrock was fairly well represented), the day itself was a disappointment. The event was held in a cow pasture that hadn't been properly prepared for the running, ball playing and other games of skill.

"The day ended in a drizzly rain," she remembers. "I was cold, wet and tired when I arrived at my log cabin."

To add insult to injury, on her long walk home Ethel inadvertently dropped her school register, which each participating school had to bring to prove the ages of the children. She didn't even realize it was gone until a neighbour found it on the road and brought it to her the next day. School registers were practically sacred.

"I recalled the lecture we had been given about the safekeeping of it. I felt an ugly blot on my efficiency as a teacher."

School closed in mid-August 1943. Ethel's baby was due in just a few weeks and she would not return to Woodrock. Once again the school was teacherless and, as it turned out, remained so for a long time to come.

Ethel settled into life at home. Her fourth daughter was born in early September. With a newborn, a two-year-old, a four-year-old and a six-year-old, along with all the chores of farm life, there wasn't much spare time. She did, however, manage to set aside an hour a day to practice the violin. She taught the girls to sing, and her oldest to play the organ. It was also time to give her six-year-old home instruction in grade one.

Fred got a job with the municipality so was gone most of the time. As he had to walk the twenty miles home he only came back every two weeks.

"One day when [he] came home he had encountered the teacher of the school in Hazel Dell," remembers Ethel. "She inquired if I would like to go back teaching. [By this time teaching positions were frozen because of the war.] This teacher wanted to resign and join her sister who taught at another school that had need of a teacher . . . [She] thought that if I would send in my application with her resignation, perhaps they may accept it."

Ethel and Fred discussed it.

"You don't have to go . . . but I think you are happier teaching," were Fred's words. That was all Ethel needed to hear. She applied and got the job.

The teacher was so grateful she and her family arranged for Ethel to purchase their house so that she could have a place to live in the hamlet of Hazel Dell. The mother went with the daughter to keep house for the two sisters and the father moved into a room downtown. For fifty dollars down and ten monthly payments of twenty-five dollars, Ethel had herself a home.

"At that price no one could expect much," she declares. "It wasn't much. It was two granaries pulled together."

But Ethel was used to confined spaces. Besides, within two years her husband had added on a big new house and the granaries became a woodshed.

"The doorway provided us a way to bring in wood without going outside," she remembers. "What a treat this was. Instead of digging wood out of the snow, it was dry."

Ethel couldn't move into Hazel Dell until the Labour Day weekend, so she walked four and a half miles from the farm to the school for the first few teaching days.

"Walking was no problem," she remarks, "but when [the first] morning arrived and it was raining I had my doubts . . . I set out, wondering what kind of a sorry sight I would be for my first appearance at a new school."

As it happened, Ethel had only to walk two miles. The cream truck driver came along and gave her a ride most of the way. When she got to the school the door was locked. This *was* the first day of school, wasn't it?

"I stood under the small roof over the door. It was some time before anyone else appeared. At least I hadn't made a mistake. Now I had company to await the coming of the janitor to open the door. More pupils arrived. Someone suggested that perhaps [the janitor] had not been notified. Someone offered to go and tell her. She lived a half a mile away . . . Thus the pupils and I got to know one another on the top step . . . in a very friendly atmosphere even if wet."

The janitor indeed had not been informed. She needed an interpreter to explain to Ethel that the school was not ready for use. Ethel convinced her to let them in anyway and the children spent the rest of the morning cleaning the school. It was an unusual way to begin the year but as Ethel says, "So what? . . . Clean-up . . . needs to be learned [too]."

Over the Labour Day weekend two of Ethel's students helped her move into Hazel Dell. With two teams and two wagons they loaded up everything, including the livestock, relocating the entire farm. The only animals that couldn't be kept in town were the two pigs. They were ensconced in a pen on the outskirts and the cow was established in a nearby pasture. By the time school resumed Tuesday morning Ethel and the children had settled right in.

Ethel started with twelve students but that didn't last. Mothers and their children were returning home to live with parents, as their husbands were sent overseas to war. The student population of Shaftesbury School in Hazel Dell soon swelled to forty-nine.

"Extra seats [were] added until there were no more aisles, only a narrow space for me to shuffle sideways to the front of the room," recalls Ethel. "The pupils scrambled over the desks to get to and from their seats."

Occasionally, in school districts throughout the country, problems with trustees necessitated school boards dissolving and the superintendent being appointed official trustee. Such was the case with Shaftesbury. When the superintendent arrived, however, it was to tell Ethel he would not be coming back.

"He . . . had too much work to do helping unqualified teachers manage their schools to be concerned about mine," she states. "I was to act as official trustee and manage the best I could."

In light of her many students, he did have one piece of advice for her before he left.

"He suggested that I dispense with exams and use my time for teaching. I would be able to evaluate pupils for what was needed without the extra burden of preparing, administering, correcting and tabulating exams."

This Ethel was happy to do. She had one grade ten correspondence student taking grade nine and ten French in one year. Ethel went out of her way to help the girl, even though she already had a huge workload with so many students. Soon the sense of something odd came over Ethel. She couldn't help but feel the girl was ungrateful. After passing her exams she moved on to high school in another town and then to Normal School. On her first visit home from Normal the girl made her way over to Ethel's, a confession and heartfelt apology on her lips.

"She told me [that] when she attended Normal School they taught her to teach like I was teaching," says Ethel. "She had told the people of Hazel Dell that I didn't know how to teach [because] I didn't teach the way her other teachers taught."

Another thing Ethel didn't do the way other teachers did was discipline. Although she knew how to use it, Ethel hated the strap.

"I found punishment only set up rebellion," she claims. "Love and understanding set up friendship."

Using this philosophy in a unique way, she "dealt with [troublemakers] one on one, in a friendly manner, talking to them until they were in tears—even large boys." This was so effective that one boy requested the strap, preferring it to the long, uncomfortable lecture. He didn't get it.

"One noontime when I was returning from home," remembers Ethel, "I saw boys jumping out of the window next to the steps . . . Jokingly I said to them, 'Oh, if that is what you like to do keep on doing it even when the bell rings. The rest of us will just go ahead with our usual work.' Soon they tired and were going to sit in their seats. 'Oh no. Keep on jumping,' [I said]. They were so tired and needed encouragement to keep on. Finally I let them quit. No anger—nor sense of punishment."

One way in which the students expressed their athleticism appropriately was at the annual sports day. This time Ethel was the teacher hosting the twelve-school event. She chose to hold it in the empty lot across from the school. Although it was wooded, she made sure the grounds were more suitably prepared than the pasture had been the year she taught at Woodrock.

By late spring of 1945 soldiers were returning home from the war. It was decided that a memorial hall be built in their honour. The lot across from the school was chosen and Fred and Ethel became heavily involved in the fundraising and construction. The hall was finished in time for Ethel to hold the school Halloween party there as well as the Christmas program. In the spring of 1946 she anticipated an even better sports day. Wouldn't it be wonderful to have a proper playing ground beside the new hall? She approached the municipality, asking for permission to make improvements to the site.

"They didn't only give permission," she relates, "they sent their municipal machines and cleared the land of trees! This met with opposition. It would have been nice to have had some trees and shrubbery left."

Denuded of trees, the grounds were an open field. They easily accommodated the 300 students, twelve teachers and innumerable spectators who arrived for the annual event. But they couldn't provide shelter when the rain began to fall. Thank goodness for the new hall, which also housed the concession booth, held indoors for the first time. The sports day was a washout, but the booth was a sellout. It had to be restocked for their second attempt two days later. This time the field was in top shape. The mud had dried, leaving a smooth, hard surface onto which Ethel chalked lines for the various events.

"We had more spectators," she observes. "Everyone seemed to be in a joyous mood. We had put our new building to a worthwhile use."

By now Ethel had five children and was still teaching. Her two oldest were in school with her and the other three in the care of an excellent sitter. She stayed at Shaftesbury School until 1949 when she transferred to Glenside to be near her dying parents.

When her doctor advised her in 1950 that she must either give up teaching or give up housework, Ethel resigned her position, determined to devote herself to husband and family. Two months later she was back in school.

Why?

"My own children, after spending time in another classroom, begged me to get a school of our own," she explains. "I did, and taught another twenty-one years!"

Terry

"I have to say I was much more prepared for country living after my experiences as a supervisor and the first year of teaching. I certainly kept more food in the house and never failed to listen to weather reports . . ."

Those are the pearls of wisdom Terry Trentham (known in 1947 as Miss Theresa McLellan) learned the hard way. When she moved roughly thirty miles from her Drumheller home at age nineteen to supervise correspondence lessons in a country school she had never known anything but city life. She didn't have a clue about fires or about having to walk five miles for groceries. She wasn't used to not having a phone and being isolated even from neighbours. Coming from a family of twelve, she had never lived alone. She'd never even done much cooking, as she had always been the designated baby-sitter instead.

What she lacked in experience was made up for in enthusiasm. She'd always wanted to be a teacher but couldn't afford Normal School. She was thrilled to have a chance to get practical experience while making money to finance her goal.

The Greenleaf School near Three Hills, Alberta had only five students. Terry saw that as an advantage.

"I had lots of time . . . to preview the lessons and give myself the background in Science, Social Studies, Health, Art, Reading,

Writing and Math," she states. "These courses introduced me to many . . . methods of teaching . . . even though I was only supervising . . . There were twenty lessons, [two per month], all to be completed on time and sent to the Department of Education. They were corrected and sent back and I was to go over all the corrections with each student . . . It was a wonderful start for me. I learned so much from those correspondence courses."

She also learned a lot about country living. Terry occupied a two-room teacherage. Alone, with no phone, she found time heavy on her hands. She decided to take a correspondence course herself. Latin lessons helped her while away many evening hours. But she was extremely lonely. When she could get to a phone she phoned her father. His car wasn't reliable, but the man who ran the telephone office had a good car. Together they came up and brought Terry home for the weekend.

For a while she also had a welcome visitor.

"My mother was expecting her thirteenth child in November. My father brought my younger sister Pat [aged five] with him when it was close to the date the new baby would be born . . . She loved coming over to the school with me and participating in activities suited to her. She loved to help with small chores in the school . . . She stayed until a week after the new child, Catherine, was born."

"When my parents could not visit they both corresponded by mail," observes Terry.

Her mail came to the Ghost Pine post office, where there was also a store to pick up a few groceries. Occasionally a neighbour gave Terry a ride. If not, she walked the four or five miles. It wasn't uncommon for her groceries to run low.

Terry also spent time walking for miles on country roads. At least once she walked to eleven o'clock mass at Lumini Church.

"It was five miles or more from the teacherage . . . a beautiful, clear, sunny morning with lots of light, fluffy snow," she recalls. "I was given a ride by some neighbours for the last mile and invited for lunch on the return trip."

It's a very good thing she accepted, for she says had she not she'd have been "ten feet under." A blizzard struck with sudden and terrible force. She was stranded at the neighbours' for several days before they finally got her back to the teacherage by sleigh.

Terry was often invited to the homes of parents for meals, a gesture she truly appreciated, as she was not a cook. They also gave her rides to various community events and were generally helpful in any way they could. Her closest neighbours were Hungarian and, though she had difficulty communicating with them, the man of the house was a godsend.

"Nobody taught me how to light a fire," says Terry. "I had a terrible time. But, you know, the Hungarian neighbour would come over to the school for me and build the fire in the pot-bellied stove and we'd sit around that to keep warm, because it was a bigger school than they needed for five students."

In fact, to Terry the almost empty school seemed huge.

The people of the district expected a Christmas concert, even though Terry was just a supervisor with so few students. She was quite concerned about it until she realized they weren't going to leave her high and dry.

"I had met enough young women in the community who were quite willing to be involved in the singing, poetry and plays. We had a great time planning and organizing the concert . . . Somehow we even managed to get help in the music area. Some of the local people played guitars."

After the concert Terry found a ride home to Drumheller for Christmas, but when it came time to head back to Greenleaf her brother wasn't taking any chances. He hired a taxi and travelled back with her himself to "make sure I got there safely."

"I don't remember what the bill was because I didn't have to pay for it," says Terry. "It probably would've taken half my cheque. But I think he knew the taxi driver."

That winter another blizzard caught Terry off guard. It raged for days and her food supplies became very low.

"I had neighbours who lived within walking distance but the blizzard was too wicked to even step outside the door."

She tried to keep herself apprised of the storm by listening to her radio, but she had to be careful not to keep it on too long because she had no extra batteries.

"After two or three days a neighbour came on her horse to see how I was surviving and I had only jelly to serve her . . . She brought some fudge as a treat for us."

When the storm was finally over "roads were completely blocked for miles around" and Terry was literally snowed in.

"The snowbanks in front of the teacherage were almost as high as the doorway and . . . I dug a tunnel over the pathway to the school."

Soon her Hungarian neighbour arrived to ensure she was all right and replenish her food and fuel. It was a frightening and isolating experience that Terry was sure couldn't have been worse. She was wrong.

In May a newly graduated Normalite came to replace her. When a teacher replaced a supervisor so late in the year correspondence lessons continued. Terry and Margaret got along well and Terry agreed to stay, helping Margaret settle in and familiarize herself with the school, the children and the district. They became good friends.

The following year Terry fulfilled her dream of attending

Normal School. Consequently, in May she was the one being sent out to replace a supervisor. At first she refused to accept White Star South School, only ten miles from her home. She'd heard some "weird" stories about it, one of which involved the students locking the supervisor in the coal bin. Her superintendent told Terry that if she could teach at White Star South she could teach anywhere. So Terry decided to accept the challenge.

To her surprise she found the twelve students "enthusiastic and well-behaved." Two were taking grade nine by correspondence and she helped them just as she had the students at Greenleaf. Government departmental exams made grade nine a crucial year. One very bright girl was struggling under all the responsibilities and distractions she had at home with her large family. With her parents' permission, Terry took the girl home to Drumheller on weekends. There she made sure she had the solitude needed for extra study.

The time for departmental exams arrived. There were strict regulations. They must be written on a certain day, they must begin on the dot of 9:00, they must be closely supervised with no interruptions and they must be turned in at a specified hour.

"I knew the rules," asserts Terry, "but the day the exams were being written we looked out of the school windows and there was a grass fire!"

Thoughts of testing vanished while students and teacher alike ran for all the water they had and dashed out to quell the flames. Dousing and stamping the scorched earth, they finally succeeded in preventing a prairie fire.

"Back to our places to finish the exam," states Terry. "Of course we didn't consider our fire 'unforeseen circumstances'— just a recess break—and not serious enough to report to the Department of Education."

In September Terry told the school board that she would only return to White Star South School if they provided her with a piano. They did. This time Terry's sister, Mary, joined her to attend school and live in the teacherage.

"She was in grade six piano," remembers Terry, "so would accompany us in the music area . . . Mrs. Jakey left songs for her to use for . . . music lessons."

The Drumheller Rural School Division Supervisor of Instruction, Mrs. Jakey, was Terry's biggest help and inspiration.

"Though we had experienced practice teaching in Normal School we needed so much help with so many grades in the one-room school. The first week she came out she taught some sample lessons on different subjects and in different grades . . . Timetables were a real pain . . . and I really appreciated it when Mrs. Jakey offered to help with them."

Supervisors of Instruction were not unique to Alberta. Their Saskatchewan counterparts were 'Helping Teachers'. Margaret Tjeltveit (now Sillerud) was a Helping Teacher in the Swift Current School Unit. She recalls that they were needed because "the post war shortage of teachers necessitated the use of grade twelve graduates to supervise . . . correspondence courses. Also, there were teachers pressured back to the classroom after upwards to twenty-five years away, [and] each year also brought a new batch of graduates from training."

Margaret visited two schools a day, driving up to sixty miles to assist teachers with any concerns they had, either with the curriculum or with how to organize a one-room school.

"Another aspect of the job [was] the development of a lending library," she states.

Mabel Hobbs remembers what an advantage it was to be able to choose titles from a long list of books and have them shipped out, postage paid, to be kept in the school for three or four weeks before sending back. Margaret also helped restore existing collections in rural schools. As she points out, "few books had been purchased in the pioneer era, the thirties or the war years."

For Terry's part, she "always looked forward to Mrs. Jakey's visits . . . as she always brought along more ideas and materials . . . and books when possible."

The older boys at White Star South had ideas too. A monthly news bulletin was a lot of fun! Local stories liberally interspersed with jokes filled up two or three pages.

"You can imagine the work this took on a hectograph," comments Terry. "The only paper we had was the brown newsprint so we had to be very careful when pulling the copies up off the pad as the paper was very thin."

The boys were proud of their efforts and even printed programs for the Christmas concert. Again Terry had a lot of help. Even though many of the mothers couldn't speak English they were eager to lend a hand. Their children translated in Hungarian or Czechoslovakian and everything came together beautifully.

"I shall never forget this concert and the fun we had getting ready for it," smiles Terry. "Unknown to me, there was a guest in the audience, Bob Trentham, who many years later became my husband."

The only disturbance of the evening took place when three children from one family arrived late. Terry's heart wrenched each time she laid eyes on these beautiful, blue-eyed angels. Clearly they were neglected. They were "very poor and uncared for and the parents often left them alone to go to town."

Terry had already stepped in to rescue them once. One of the boys had raced across the field one day to bang on her teacherage door.

"[He asked] me to come over to the home as his baby sister was very sick," Terry anguishes. "When we arrived I couldn't believe how ill the baby was and the state of the crib she was lying in—wet, neglected, and in need of a bath, clean clothes and food. I cared for them all until the parents arrived home."

Now the three older children came to the concert in need of attention again.

"The parents . . . were not home to wash or dress them . . . so over to the teacherage to wash and comb [their] hair. As soon as we got back to the school my brother, who acted as chairman, began the concert . . . My washed clean family performed very well."

The whole time Terry served White Star South School these young ones benefited from her care and compassion.

"My parents were unaware," she says, "that when Mary and I left home each weekend and returned to the teacherage . . . these children would show up through rain, snow or sunshine and partake of . . . food and hot chocolate—in winter sometimes with no mittens or boots."

The teacherage and school were situated beside a dirt trail in the river valley. When the wind blew, so did the dirt, both off the trail and from the hilltops. One spring morning Terry and her sister were appalled to wake to "layers of dirt on the bedcovers and throughout the teacherage."

They shared a bed in the two-room dwelling and were lucky to have a pot-bellied stove in the bedroom for heat. But Terry was still learning to manage fires. One night they had a close call.

"The stove was very close to the bed and because I had not banked it carefully it became red and overheated. One had to bank the fire with the slower burning bone coal to keep it going, but if not banked properly we could have nothing but smoke in the place."

Another close call came when their coal oil lamp accidentally set ablaze the curtains and paper tablecloth. Fire was an ever-present hazard. One night Terry woke to a shocking sight. Through her window glowed the flame-engulfed remains of a nearby house. It belonged to a teacher she knew who taught at a school several miles away. The woman's husband burned to death in the blaze.

"This was a terrible tragedy in that community," she laments.

Before leaving White Star South to move on to Manor School the next year, Terry did something many in the region never forgot.

"There was at least one Catholic mother who had never attended church since she had left Hungary," Terry relates, "so I contacted a Hungarian priest who came out and said mass in the school . . . This was set up like a retreat where short talks were given in Hungarian."

Terry remarks that "the families really appreciated being involved, especially the mothers," but it is doubtful she'll ever know just how much this kind gesture meant to them.

Manor School was eight miles east and one mile south of Three Hills. Situated in a more affluent area, it was larger and more modern than her previous schools, but not necessarily a happier place to be. The people were friendly enough, and just as cooperative as they had been at White Star South and Greenleaf, but Terry felt they expected a great deal more from her. She had the sense of being watched and made a careful point of visiting all seven of her families to minimize the risk of incurring criticism or offence.

The situation was made more sensitive by her close association with the family of the chairman of the school board. As it happened, his oldest children were her age and they belonged to the same church.

"We became very good friends," Terry remembers. "I spent weekends in this home if we travelled to dances or young people's meetings. Whenever the board chairman had a divisional meeting in Drumheller I had a ride home."

Naturally, people wondered if there was favouritism afoot. One unfortunate Friday Terry dismissed the school early because she was catching a ride with the chairman to Drumheller. After she dismissed the children, but before they arrived home, an unforeseen dust storm blew up. Black blizzards were as treacherous as white blizzards for reduced visibility and even more so for the powerfully abrasive, sandpaper-like quality of their blowing grit. Thankfully, all the children made it home unharmed.

"As would be expected," says Terry, "there were many complaints on my leaving early on that particular day, even though the chairman of the board was in agreement and the children were safe."

Another time Terry arrived home very late after a Catholic Youth Organization dance in Three Hills. The friend who gave her a ride got stuck in the snow outside her teacherage.

"We spent some time shovelling in order to get out," she recalls. "I noticed a light on in one of the students' homes on a hill around a mile away. I often wondered if they really knew what had happened on this occasion and what we were doing at these odd hours in the morning."

Again Terry lived in a two-room teacherage, by herself this time. It was exceptionally cold.

"The small stove in the kitchen did not provide enough heat even at its best so I often slept with many layers of clothes, a hot-water bottle to start with, and then pitching it out when it became too cold to stand any longer. Keeping the old stove hot enough but not so hot that it would burn the small, shell-like teacherage down took lots of practice."

The school had a wooden water pump in the basement from which Terry hauled water across the yard to the teacherage. She also carried coal from the school.

"If I didn't get home for a weekend," she observes, "I would have to heat water for a round-tub sponge bath, wash my sheets, clothes, and lastly the floor before I threw the water out."

In the spring the worst blizzard yet descended on the little teacherage. This time Terry "heard the storm warnings on the radio."

"I was fearful of what might happen with no phone or any connection to the people around. Those living the closest I had not . . . seen very often so felt they did not want to be involved with the teacher."

Terry did her best to prepare. She carried extra water and coal from the school, but still she underestimated the severity of what was to come.

"I was unable to leave the teacherage," she recalls, "and through the side bedroom window I could see the snow building up higher and higher . . . after the third day I was low on coal and only had a kettle of hot water left."

Terry had no choice but to attempt to get to the school for these two essentials.

"After tripping and falling a few times I made it over there only to find the school door was totally frozen, hinges and all. I went back for the kettle of hot water in order to melt the ice off the handles and hinges. After chipping and pulling I finally opened the door and went down to the basement where the pump was situated. Frozen solid!"

With no water to be had, Terry filled her pail with coal. The trip back to the teacherage was just as gruelling, made worse by the disappointment of the fruitless efforts with the pump. Part way there she tripped and dumped her coal. She lay in the snow, tears welling up in her eyes.

"I felt so alienated, angry and helpless! Like what kind of a crazy life is this?"

There was nothing to do but struggle on. She picked up what coal she could and fought her way back to the teacherage. Lesson planning and marking helped her pass the time. So did a large cross-stitch project. The stifling feeling of isolation was eased by the radio, but in the dire circumstances even the radio was a source of distress. Terry was stricken to hear that a river-bank avalanche had buried the small home of a dear friend of hers.

"The news report mentioned that their baby girl had not lived through the ordeal," she grieves. "A neighbour rescued the mother who had to be taken to the nearest hospital with severe frostbite. Her husband . . . was away getting supplies and was unable to get home because of the blizzard so . . . was unaware of what was happening to his wife and child."

Terry couldn't stand it any longer. She had to get out. By now it wasn't blowing so badly so she set off towards the home of one of her students. She didn't know that the chairman's wife had already sent her grown son to come for Terry. He was walking the five miles and happened to stop for a break at the same place for which Terry was heading.

"The Mrs. had just made fresh bread so we were delighted to share bread and jam with the family," she recalls.

Then Terry proceeded with the son to the chairman's home and stayed until the storm was over and the roads cleared.

Even with the isolation and hardship of her first three years in a one-room school, Theresa McLellan never lost her enthusiasm for teaching. She went on to St. Mary's Girls School in Calgary, as well as the separate system in Windsor, Ontario. In 1956 she and Bob were married and from their union sprang five children, all now high-level professionals in fields related to education. After raising her family Terry returned to teaching, finally retiring in 1985.

If it hadn't been for the opportunity first to be an untrained supervisor, she never would've become a teacher. She had been accepted at the Misericordia Hospital in Edmonton for nurse's training when she learned of the plight of rural schools and the supervisory program.

"This meant that I could . . . earn money to pursue the career I knew I would love and leave the nursing career to those most suited for it. My father . . . breathed a sigh of relief as he knew what I really wanted to do with my life."

Lenore

 Terry wanted to be a teacher, but applied to nursing school when she thought she couldn't do it. By contrast, Lenore Warkentine wanted to be a nurse, but applied to become a permit teacher instead. Why? She was missing one subject for nursing school, and her sister Lorene, already a permit teacher, was having such a wonderful time that she encouraged Lenore to follow in her footsteps.

Lorene was a natural teacher; Lenore had misgivings. After Lenore was hired for the Wigton School near Glenora, Manitoba she, Lorene, and Lorene's fiancé went to meet the people Lenore was to board with. They visited for perhaps an hour, then went to take a look at the schoolhouse, which was never locked.

Lenore didn't have the heart to express her doubts to Lorene. Her sister, older by two years, had always been a positive influence. When their rural schooling ended in grade eight it was at Lorene's incentive that they continued by correspondence until grade eleven. Her enthusiasm was contagious and Lenore did love children. Perhaps she'd enjoy being a permit teacher after all!

In 1947 Lenore had just turned seventeen and she'd never been out on her own.

Looking back now she reflects with wonder: "I was just a babe."

Her landlady was quick to advise her that if she wasn't home in time for meals there wouldn't be any. She had five hungry young mouths to feed and it was first come first served.

That was fine by Lenore until she realized how much extra work she'd have at the school.

"I stayed until it was dark," she says, "putting work on the board and getting organized for the next day. I had to, because if I came to school in the morning and there were no preparations made . . . "

She shudders to think of it. So night after night she walked the mile back to her boarding house to find supper gone, just as the landlady had warned.

"I fried myself an egg or made myself some toast," she says. "I was a skinny little thing in those days."

Lenore taught solely by instinct and imitation.

"I had absolutely no training," she reveals. "I was just plunked into this school."

She had attended three different country schools herself, so had several examples to follow. Her main recollection was an emphasis on Penmanship and English so she stressed those at Wigton. She also held lots of spelling bees, an activity she used to love as a student. Of course there was a curriculum guide to follow but very few books for supplemental material.

"I searched right through that library to see what I could dig up to teach the different grades," she recalls.

The job was formidable in more ways than one. The school was loaded with mice!

"Every book in this little library—which was really in a porch—were mice-chewed, and there were droppings all over everything. It was actually quite ugly."

Feeling utterly revolted, Lenore wiped everything up.

Fortunately, she never laid eyes on any of the hated creatures.

"As long as there were people in the school they didn't bother us. It was just at night they all came out of hiding."

Mice weren't the only thing Lenore found bothersome. She had two male students older than she was. They were brothers, taking grade nine and ten respectively by correspondence. They weren't passing. They weren't even doing the work. In fact it was their third year of the same courses.

"Their father had nothing for them to do on the farm and he thought they might as well go to school," says Lenore. "They sat there and watched me and it made me uneasy because they weren't learning anything. They were just sitting there taking it all in."

Finally Lenore complained to the inspector.

"He came and took a look at the situation and suggested they drop out, which they did."

Mr. Lockhart was a wonderful man, supportive in every way. Lenore called upon him several times and he never failed to make himself available. He was a boon to the young girl with her twenty-plus charges.

The families of the district were extremely poor. Lenore watched her children eating sandwiches of homemade bread with wild plum jam and wondered how she could provide them with something hot. Asking them each to bring twenty-five cents a week for ingredients was futile. Instead they brought potatoes and roasted them in the hot coals of the Booker Heater (like Laura's, it had a mind of its own when it came to whether or how much it would burn). Lenore supplied butter for the steaming potatoes, but it didn't stop there. Although she made only sixty-nine dollars a month, from which she paid thirty-five dollars room and board, she spent her own money on food for the children.

"I started up a credit account at the store in Glenora and at the end of every month when I got paid I'd pay up the bill. I bought soups and we even had ice cream on occasion. I went into the hole on that one. But it was so nice just to see the children eating."

Lenore's students kept her on her toes. One little girl often fainted.

"I propped her up and put something cold on her forehead. Her sister would say, 'She'll be okay in a few minutes.' But after that she was very pale and listless."

Lenore never did learn what was wrong.

Another child was uncooperative and "just plain naughty." Lenore kept him in at recess to give him extra instruction but she soon received an admonishing note from his mother. Her son needed his fresh air and sunshine, it said. He was to go out for recess. Lenore yielded and the boy failed his grade.

"He was the only one that failed," she states.

At the other end of the scale but just as vexing was a grade two student who was exceptionally bright.

"I just couldn't keep that child busy," she recalls. "I thought, 'Why don't you slow down?'"

Lenore was getting discouraged. She was putting in hundreds of extra hours, then walking home in the dark, on feet that felt like "two clumps of ice," to missed suppers at a place that was draining over half her wage for room and board. She had so little money left to show for her efforts that her mother was sending extra money and clothes to get by. On top of it all, when Lorene got married later in the fall and Lenore was her bridesmaid, she had to pay someone from the next town to substitute for her the two days she was gone.

"This is ridiculous!" she declared. "I'm quitting!"

But Lorene replied, "Don't you dare! We don't quit! You keep on going!"

There *were* bright spots.

"We would go whooping down the country road banging on tin cans," Lenore chuckles. "I was teaching the children to march."

They won first place at the Field Day, even though it meant Lenore loaning out several of her white blouses so everybody matched. One blouse never did find its way back to her.

Another highlight was the Christmas concert. Lenore worked extra hard to produce a good one. The people of the district were suitably impressed.

"It was the best Christmas concert they'd had in years," she beams.

The greatest bright spot of all almost didn't happen. One day Lenore's landlady announced, "You have to come with us tonight to a veteran's welcome home dance."

It was an extra special occasion because the veteran, Dave Loewen, was well liked in the community. Lenore, as clothes conscious as every seventeen-year-old, declined because she had "nothing new to wear." She soon learned attendance wasn't optional.

"You *have* to come," insisted the landlady.

Lenore will never forget what she wore that night.

"I hated that old yellow plaid skirt!"

Of course we all know what happened next. "It was love at first fright," she laughs. Dave and Lenore were married five years later.

Meeting Dave clearly made up for all the reservations about permit teaching that year. Lenore is thankful now that Lorene wouldn't let her quit. Lorene Stepaniuk was certainly no quitter.

With a grade eleven education she went straight from permit teaching to working in a town school as librarian. She worked in that capacity for many years before taking full retirement from the Department of Education at age sixty.

But then, "she enjoyed it," says Lenore. "And looking back I think I probably did too—but it *was* a real struggle."

Marjorie

Marjorie Ingell recalls that in September of 1946 the girls at Saskatoon Normal School were "quite happy to see an influx of males into what had been an almost entirely female school." Veterans back from the war were trickling in, but still there weren't enough teachers.

"We could not take the full year of training," explains Marjorie. "We had a choice of going for six weeks . . . or six months before going out to teach. I chose . . . six months."

By the middle of February she wasn't sure she was ready for the Lynwood School near Shell Lake, Saskatchewan.

"Picture me in that classroom my first day," she suggests. "Twenty-nine students in grades one to ten. I was nineteen-years-old, no experience, six months training and two weeks of practice teaching in a city school."

She's quick to point out that there was no principal. Neither were there secretaries, aides, or other teachers to bounce ideas from. Marjorie simply had to handle matters as best she could. She had families of Ukrainian, English, Cree and Metis origin.

"Some of the Cree and Metis homes were shacks with dirt floors and piles of straw for beds," she comments. "Two little brothers were never very clean when they came to school. When I attempted to send a note home to ask their mother to wash them before . . . school, one of them said, 'She can't read', the other one said, 'Please, Miss Redden, we have no soap!'"

Parents who couldn't read English were the least of Marjorie's worries. Many couldn't even speak it, and consequently their children had trouble too. Marjorie was frustrated that with so many students in so many grades she only had time to work on the basics. She would've loved to have been able to show them so much more.

One student was fifteen years old and only in grade two. His frustrations were often taken out on the schoolground.

"One day I caught him hitting the other kids," says Marjorie, "and discovered he had [an iron rod] in his hand."

Her actions were swift, decisive and strictly by the book.

"I suspended him from school for two days [and] notified his parents and the local school board."

The next day Marjorie was surprised to see the boy return to school. She intercepted him at the door and turned him around. Did he not understand the meaning of the word suspension?

After school his father was waiting for Marjorie at her boarding house door.

"He demanded to know why I didn't just give [the boy] a licking like the other teachers did."

It suddenly dawned on her why the child was such a discipline problem.

"The poor boy had been beaten so much it had no effect on him . . . After the suspension he caused no more trouble."

Marjorie also understood why his father did not want him suspended from school. In 1944 the federal government had instituted Family Allowances. The rule was that if a child missed more than a certain number of school days each month his or her allotment was withheld. For many it was a strong incentive to make sure their children were in school.

Marjorie was touched when she learned some time after the incident that the other students were afraid for her when she confronted the iron-wielding bully.

"They were prepared to protect me," she exclaims.

The children liked Marjorie. Who wouldn't like a teacher who held a "little party" during the last period at the end of almost every school week?

"They liked to sing and I can't," she remarks. "We had to learn to play [the tonette] at Normal School. So I played my tonette to teach them new songs. One boy played the fiddle by ear and I taught them some square dances."

The Field Day in Shell Lake was much anticipated for the students of Lynwood School were strong athletes. The ten-mile trip to get there, however, was a problem. None of the children's parents owned a vehicle.

"One man in the district had a big truck," remembers Marjorie, "but he wanted five dollars to take us."

There was no way Marjorie would ask that of the parents, whom she knew to be very poor. She approached the school board, but they wouldn't pay. She would've proffered the money herself—if she had it. Finally the matter was settled.

"Two of the fathers offered to take us with teams of horses and wagons—lumber wagons, not rubber-tired ones. If I remember right, we did very well at the Field Day and it rained on the way home!"

Marjorie had only her own two feet to get her to the little school nestled "in a clearing in the bush." If she took the road it was a five-mile walk but if she followed the tracks it was only a mile and a half. Naturally she chose the tracks, even though a trestle bridge over a lake part way posed a risk.

"I walked on the ties and looked down between them to the water below," she quivers. "A little scary . . . "

But not as scary as being caught on the trestle when a train came. Marjorie was always careful to check both ways before stepping onto the bridge. One morning she was a third of the way across when she heard a noise behind her. Section men speeding up the track on a jigger!

"I had to run to the halfway mark where a sort of cage had been built out from the track for just such emergencies."

Even though it was generally against regulations, the men stopped and offered Marjorie a ride to the point nearest the school. It was exciting.

"My first ride on a jigger!"

It's too bad there was no ride the day of the heavy spring snowfall.

"I walked that mile and a half up the railroad track in snow up to my knees. No jeans or slacks for teachers in those days. I had to take my stockings off when I got to the school and hang them over the tin barricade [surrounding the barrel stove] to dry."

Marjorie lived with the lady who ran the store and post office from her home. No doubt it was very convenient for the locals to check her out when she first arrived. Did they consider how convenient it was for Marjorie to check them out too?

From her $100 a month she paid thirty-five dollars room and board. She was quite happy with her upstairs bedroom and even felt grateful for the bologna sandwiches she got in her lunch day after day after day.

"Some of the children had only bannock," she explains.

There wasn't a lot of entertainment.

"My landlady had a radio and we listened to the Amateur Hour from Prince Albert every Saturday night."

Marjorie also walked for hours in the beautiful countryside.

"Some of us walked to Shell Lake one night to a dance and got a ride home on a tractor!"

Another time they went to a "picture show" in an old truck. There were a few anxious moments.

"The floorboards were apparently too close to the exhaust," points out Marjorie. "They caught fire several times on the way. Not to worry! [My friends] stopped, removed the floorboards, stomped out the fire, replaced them and [we] went on our way."

By the end of June Marjorie had four months of teaching behind her. That, combined with a good inspector's report and her six months of training, qualified her for an Interim Teaching Certificate. By now she was "very fond of the children and it was hard to leave."

In fact she was asked to stay. She couldn't pass up the offer of a school closer to home, however. She sadly said goodbye to her first young scholars—and an introduction to teaching that she'll never forget!

Margaret

Ray Petrowski stood before the class with gum on his nose for a full five minutes. He also stood a full head taller than his seventeen-year-old supervisor. Margaret MacArthur stood for no nonsense and chewing gum in school was nonsense.

In 1950 supervisors were still needed to oversee correspondence lessons in rural schools. She'd been hand-picked for the Lake Alice School twenty-five miles northeast of her Viking, Alberta home. They'd had trouble with discipline there and since Margaret had already done some substitute teaching in Viking they thought she could handle the job. Margaret suspects that being the oldest of a large family of boys had something to do with it as well.

The fact of the matter was that Margaret, who just finished grade eleven, had been thinking of quitting school and going out to work anyway. Her high school teacher was dead set against it.

"[He] was very determined that I . . . graduate with university entrance," she recalls.

When the opportunity came for her to supervise he saw it as the best of both worlds.

"He said I'd have no problem taking grade twelve by correspondence while supervising. It was true. He also offered help with the lessons if I needed it."

Margaret accepted the position.

"The superintendent of the Holden School District picked me up at my parents' home and drove me to Lake Alice School ... From there he drove me to the home of Mr. and Mrs. Hanson, with whom I would have room and board . . . As the superintendent drove away I was struck by the fact that I would have to walk nearly two miles to and from the school. Up until now I had only two blocks to go to attend school . . . grades one [through] eleven. The enormity of what I had taken on began to register . . ."

The superintendent told Margaret that the correspondence lessons wouldn't arrive for another week. He suggested in the meantime she "just review the previous year's work." How was she going to do that with fifteen students in nine grades?

"I was very thankful for the teachers I'd had," she comments. "Spelling and Arithmetic bees were very much part of our schooling. So that's what we did for the first one and a half weeks. As it turned out I think it was a good beginning, as I was able to determine where each student was with the basics.

Margaret discovered that in the predominantly Ukrainian community the former teacher had spoken Ukrainian to the students. One little boy could hardly speak a word of English. He was in grade two but hadn't finished his grade one lessons yet. Margaret spent extra time with him on both his English and his lessons and brought him a long way in the year. She also helped the other students with their English. In one instance this backfired.

When winter came she was often picked up on her snowy walk to school by a man who drove his children by sleigh.

"One day," she recalls, "he passed me by, with the snow just a-flying. I was covered with it. When I reached school he followed me inside, shook his fist at me, and said, 'See here, Missy Teacher.' Then a string of words in his own language. I couldn't figure out what was wrong. Later, my landlord found out that I had been trying too hard to teach the man's children good English, and he didn't want them to become 'too educated'!"

Margaret was not the strict disciplinarian everybody thought she was. In truth, the day she made Ray stand with gum on his nose she was quaking. He was a six-foot-tall, fifteen-year-old farm boy! Margaret doesn't know how she kept discipline.

"All the students were obedient even though three of the boys were taller than I was and almost as old."

She learned years later that they had no idea how young she was.

Margaret was settling in and feeling as though things were working rather well when the students advised her it was almost time for the annual Junior Red Cross dance.

"Oh?" she commented. "Who organizes that?"

"You do!" they chorused.

"I felt my knees going weak!"

To her great consternation Margaret was in charge of arranging everything—the music, the lunch and preparing the schoolroom. A country dance was a new experience for the town girl. Fortunately, the students helped.

"I found they had four men who played the music and the women brought lunch. The desks were pushed back and we danced from 9:00 PM until about 3:00 AM."

It was both an enlightening evening and a great success!

"I had just heaved a sigh of relief that it was over when one of the mothers reminded me that we should be practicing for the Christmas concert."

Here we go again!

Margaret had to think about this one. The school had a piano but she couldn't play it. Even if she could, where would she get the music? Or other items for the program? Then she had an idea.

"The Viking United Church ladies . . . gave me copies of a suitable Christmas play . . . Christmas songs and memory verses."

Again Margaret cast back in her memory to her own school days. Her early teachers had been very good at staging the annual event so she emulated them as much as she could. She also found a lady who would play the piano.

"[She] rode horseback five miles each way twice a week so we could practice."

Every teacher is anxious on the night of the concert, but Margaret was "a bundle of nerves."

"I felt the children didn't do as well as they had at practice," she confides, "and of course [they] couldn't resist waving to the audience, laughing, etc. When we were having lunch afterwards some of the parents told me it was the best concert they'd ever had! I was amazed!"

Margaret was surprised by her feelings when she returned home for Christmas. The things she'd always taken for granted were suddenly very special.

"It was so wonderful to be able to walk downtown again," she thrills, "see all my friends, go to social functions, etc."

She realized that she didn't want to return to Lake Alice School. But she'd made a commitment. As with Lenore, quitting was out of the question.

"I knew I had to finish the job. As my dad and I were driving back to the school I was struck by . . . how bleak the farms, animals and trees looked."

It didn't take long for Margaret to get back into the spirit of things. A big help were the festivities of the Ukrainian/Polish Christmas and New Year. Margaret was included in the gaiety and thoroughly enjoyed herself.

"Those people knew how to make their own fun!" she exclaims.

It tempered the bitter winter with its relentless snow. Roads were hard to keep open and often not maintained. On farms and in fields some animals froze to death.

"One thing that impressed me greatly," remembers Margaret, "was that the children always got to school, so I went too, no matter how cold it was."

Margaret certainly missed the vibrant life teenagers in town enjoyed. Viking was building a new arena and to raise funds they held a monthly dance. Margaret so wanted to attend! One day when she heard the dance advertised on the radio she came up with an elaborate plan. If she could somehow get eight miles to the nearest phone and call her dad, perhaps he would drive the other seventeen miles out to get her.

The plan involved cooperation from several people. First Margaret's landlord took her one and a half miles by sled to the nearest neighbour. He had a "motorized type of sleigh" with which he took her the next six and a half miles to the farm with the phone.

"The people were very kind," recalls Margaret. "I phoned my dad who said he thought it was impossible for him to get to where I was. But he'd try."

Her hopes soared. She was halfway to making it to the dance! The man with the motorized sleigh waited to make sure her dad arrived. Two hours later the phone rang.

"Dad [had] gotten stuck and had to walk to get help to get himself out," she says.

There would be no dance that night. Margaret was despondent. She had tried so hard and so many people had gone out of their way for her. The man with the 'snowmobile' took her back to her boarding place. It was 6:00 AM by the time they arrived.

"Nobody teased me much," she reflects, "but I knew they all thought I was nuts to have tried that trip!"

Spring was very welcome that year—until Margaret learned for the first time of the gruesome practice of gopher killing. She was shocked when the boys told her about it and asked permission to do it on school grounds.

"Certainly not!" was her response.

She had never even seen a gopher, let alone seen one killed. She couldn't stand the thought of it. Within a day the notes from parents began arriving, telling her to "let the kids kill the gophers. They were a plague and the children got paid for each . . . tail."

Margaret let them do it. As a teenage supervisor her clear choice was simply to do as she was told.

The preferred method of extermination was waiting for the gopher to pop out of its hole, then banging it on the head with a board. Margaret couldn't bear to watch. One day an executioner's accomplice put his head too close to the hole and got the full force of the board treatment himself. Margaret was horribly frightened. Here was an injured student in her care and she had no knowledge whatsoever of first aid! Fortunately, Peter was all right, but the gopher nightmare wasn't over.

One afternoon the children simply wouldn't behave. Margaret became more and more frustrated until she was forced to announce, "I've never opened the strap drawer, but if this keeps up, I'll have to use the strap!"

It kept up.

Bursting with righteous "I-told-you-so," Margaret jerked open the strap drawer.

"To my horror there was a dead gopher in [there]! I screamed and screamed until they were all standing around my desk pleading with me to stop screaming and they finally took the dead gopher away. We played softball for the rest of the afternoon!"

Gopher capers aside, Margaret developed a deep affection for the children, the extent of which even she didn't realize until late April when she prepared to leave. A "newly graduated teacher" was coming to take her place.

"I knew 'my children' liked me [too]," she affirms, "as they had a party for me before I left."

Fifty years later Margaret (MacArthur) Scully "[looks] back on Lake Alice School [as] . . . a very pleasant memory."

Others have memories too. Recently Ray Petrowski visited her in her Kelowna, British Columbia home.

"I guess he's not angry with me over the gum incident," she winks.

Murray

. . . .
. . . .

 In his most recently dated surviving letter home from overseas during the war, my father, Flying Officer Murray Robison, comments: "I'm only here to do what part I can towards a better world in which to live. I never was, I never am, and I never will be a soldier. As soon as this mess is over I'll be the first to clamour for a good peaceful life in civvy street, teaching somewhere in a schoolroom in Alberta."

In fact Murray knew just which schoolroom he wanted. The beginning of the war in 1939 had also heralded the beginning of his term of service with the Coaldale Consolidated School. Now he wanted nothing more than to go back there.

When Murray received his discharge in November 1945 his first order of business was visiting the superintendent of the Lethbridge School Division. There he learned that there would be no openings in Coaldale until September of 1946, but if Murray would take the McLean School east of Lethbridge until then, his position in Coaldale was assured. McLean was "a one-room school in a two-room schoolhouse." It was in its last year of operation and only the lower grades remained.

"I thought I could never go back to teaching six grades [in one room] again," remarks Murray, "so I looked further afield for a job, one that would serve as a stop gap until I could get into Coaldale."

The town of Gleichen needed a grade seven teacher. Murray applied and was hired on the spot. He was to begin January 2.

"Before letting [the Lethbridge Division Superintendent] know that I would not be taking the McLean position I thought it would be a good idea to go to Gleichen and get acquainted with the school," says Murray.

He didn't have a car, so had to take the train. They say bad things happen in threes. Perhaps his first mistake was pulling a fast one on the railway company.

"Men in uniform got their transportation almost for nothing," he explains.

Of course, since his discharge Murray was no longer in uniform, but the CPR didn't know that!

"I . . . put on my officer's uniform to purchase my ticket. It worked and I got a very cheap trip to Gleichen. I stayed overnight at the hotel and after seeing the school and the teachers etc., decided that this would certainly do until I could get on staff in Coaldale."

Just a shade smug, Murray returned to Lethbridge to decline the offer of the McLean School. The superintendent was furious.

"He told me in no uncertain terms that if I didn't [take McLean] I would never get a job in Coaldale," Murray cringes. "This was a bit of blackmail, but it worked. I phoned Gleichen and said that I was sorry but I would not be able to take the position after all. Naturally, I was not very popular in that area either!"

As he had before the war, Murray lived with his grandmother and aunt in Lethbridge. Back to the "cold bedroom" tucked against the slope of the hillside house! He had a reason for wanting to save money. While in England he had fallen in love and married a British girl. Now, while waiting for the government to arrange for thousands of war brides to join their husbands in Canada, setting up a home was uppermost on his mind.

It was a great advantage to live with family, but how would he get out to the country school each day?

"I knew that the school bus picked up McNalley and McLean students at the Experimental Station just out of Lethbridge," he recalls, "so I got . . . a bike and for the month of January I got up very early on those dark, cold days, got my breakfast, and cycled out to the farm to catch the bus with the rest of [the] students."

This was rather impractical. Bicycles were a poor form of transportation in mid-winter and the bus deposited Murray and his Experimental Station students at school well before the closer pupils who walked arrived. Murray decided he needed a car. His cousin had married a mechanic. Ray was quite willing to look for a deal for Murray and soon he was driving a black 1938 Buick.

"This meant I could now get up much later and also pick up the Experimental Station students and get to school at a much more reasonable time. Everyone was happy with this arrangement!"

Indeed, the whole six months Murray taught at McLean were happy. Not only was there a janitor who always kept the school "good and warm," but Murray couldn't get over how cooperative and friendly the students and parents were.

"It seemed there was nothing they wouldn't do to make my tenure there as pleasant as possible," he exclaims. "[The year] ended with a glorious school picnic and Field Day at Henderson Lake Park which the parents organized and took complete charge of. It turned out to be one of the best six months' teaching of my career."

In August Murray's beloved Yvonne finally arrived from England and they set up house in a suite Murray had found for them in Coaldale. As the superintendent had promised, September saw Murray back at Coaldale Consolidated School teaching grade eight, the very grade he'd taught there before the war! His "good peaceful life in civvy street" was underway!

By 1948 Murray and Yvonne were well established in Coaldale. Murray was appointed vice-principal, a position he held until retirement twenty-seven years later. It came with a small raise and a huge headache.

"The biggest job was trying to balance the teachers' registers at the end of the school year," he states. "No teacher could get a cheque until his/her register balanced. Mr. Baker [the principal] and I spent hours and hours trying to straighten out some of the registers. We couldn't get our cheques either until the whole batch of [them] were done and balanced."

A big disruption in the school year took place each fall and spring when the sugar-beet fields needed hundreds of extra workers.

"In the spring the beets had to be thinned," says Murray, "and this was done by hand-hoe, up one row and down the next. In the fall the beets were handpicked and shaken to get the earth off, then thrown into a truck to be hauled to the sugar factories. Twice a year dozens and dozens of students applied for permits to be out of school to work the beets."

Some classrooms were practically empty for up to three weeks and when students returned it was very hard to catch them up on all they'd missed. Murray didn't begrudge the inconvenience. After the war thousands of European refugees had relocated to Canada.

"For some families, especially the 'new Canadians', [working the beets] was practically their only income."

Murray had always had an interest in theatre and stagecraft.

The opportunity to attend the symphony and live theatre in London during the war had fanned that interest into a bright flame. When Drama was added to the junior high curriculum as an option, and Mr. Baker decided to try it in the grade eight classroom, Murray was thrilled. They did 'The Princess and the Woodcutter'. Murray really let loose with his artistic instincts and did a weird, futuristic version of the play.

"The school certainly had no auditorium," he relates, "nor was it possible to rehearse in the community hall. All rehearsing had to be done at the back of the classroom, much to the amusement of those in the class who were not in the play. Our scenery had to be made and stored there too, much to the entertainment of the students . . . who went by the open door."

When the time came for production a temporary stage was constructed at the community hall. The play was a big success.

"From that day even to the present," says Murray, "drama has been a part of the junior high system in Coaldale."

In January of 1949 Murray and Yvonne and Mr. and Mrs. Baker planned an excursion to Calgary to see a performance of a Shakespearean play at the Old Grand Theatre. It was a special treat. Live theatre was rare in Alberta in those days. They felt it was well worth the 300-mile round trip. The plan was to leave immediately after school on the day of the event. That day dawned sunny and clear but "by ten o'clock all hell broke loose."

A raging blizzard swept in, literally out of the blue!

"When we were aware of approaching blizzards," explains Murray, "the practice was to get the school vans in as quickly as possible and get the children home. Otherwise it meant putting them up for the night in town."

The teachers scrambled to get the kids bundled up and on their way. The weather got worse and worse and was really blowing hard by the time the last van left at noon. The school was closed for the day. Murray, Yvonne and the Bakers peered out their windows and contemplated their disappointment. The storm had been furious an hour ago, but was it really so bad now? On a whim they threw caution to the wind and set out anyway.

"The blizzard petered out on the way," chuckles Murray, "and we had a fine time at the theatre and hotel overnight. We often laughed at the idea in years to come—closing the school so that we could get an early start for the trip to Calgary!"

May brought more than spring sunshine. It brought Murray and Yvonne's first pink bundle of joy. Murray's father ran the passenger train from Medicine Hat to Lethbridge and on the morning Wendy was born her euphoric father shot over to the train station at recess.

"It's a girl!" he whooped as the train whizzed past on its way to the city, the grinning new grandfather waving from the engine window.

That fall, when Wendy was six months old, Yvonne took her to England to show her off to grandparents and friends. They were gone seven months and Murray missed them dreadfully. He couldn't dwell on his misery, however. There was plenty that needed to be done.

"That was the year the teachers decided to put on a three-act play to raise money for school sports supplies," he recalls. "We chose 'The Dover Road' . . . We had to rehearse in the central hallway [of the school] . . . None of us had any training in any aspect of theatre so we just bungled our way through."

Again a makeshift stage was erected in the community hall. The play ran for two nights and was met with enthusiasm. That was the beginning of an annual event and soon the money raised was going for stage equipment instead of sports supplies. After a while so much interest was shown in the productions that Murray decided to open participation to the public. Thus was born Coaldale Little Theatre, a group nationally recognized numerous times during its twenty-three-year reign.

By 1949, with both the influx of Europeans after the war and the closure of country schools in favour of bussing to larger centres, Coaldale Consolidated School was burgeoning. Plans to build a bigger facility were well underway and the move to the new R. I. Baker School was completed in January of 1950.

Murray was delighted to have a big new gym with a proper stage from which to run the school Drama program.

"The first major project was the production of 'The Pageant of the Nations', to be presented at the formal opening of the school. The high school English teacher wrote the script for it and I did the directing. The idea was to have every ethnic group in the school represented and recognized by students of that group attending school. I set the stage with huge maple leafs and *fleur-de-lis* and lots of national flags, etc. All the participating students were dressed in their national costume and many did songs or dances representing their heritage. There were twenty-one national and ethnic groups. It was a tremendous success!"

Of "The Pageant of the Nations," the Coaldale History Book has this to say: "The new education facility was pictured as a melting pot of nations out of which came the finished product, a new Canadian."

It can also be said that the new education facility symbolized the bringing together of small country schools into larger, stronger, more effective units.

A very fitting way to end the decade. From separation to unity. From war to peace.

Born and raised in rural Alberta, ELIZABETH MCLACHLAN was inspired to write her father's memories of his experiences as a rural teacher during the Great Depression. "Several years ago I encouraged my father to write his memoirs. When I read them I was astonished by his experiences as a teacher in the Great Depression. It occurred to me that if one ordinary man had such extraordinary experiences, there must be more ordinary/extraordinary people out there. When I searched for their stories in print, however, I found almost nothing. It was then that I realized that a piece of our history had been left virtually unrecorded, and with the passage of time, was at risk of becoming lost forever."

Elizabeth McLachlan currently lives in her hometown of Coaldale, Alberta.

BY THE SAME AUTHOR:

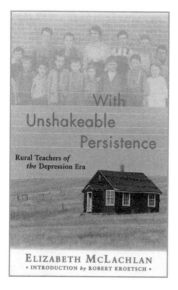

With Unshakeable Persistence
Rural Teachers of the Depression Era

Elizabeth McLachlan

With an Introduction by Robert Kroetsch

A compilation of individual stories based on the author's interviews and correspondence with several depression era teachers. Comic at times, tragic at others, together these stories tell of a past that is quickly receding from view.

"THE STORIES IN THIS BOOK ARE REMARKABLY UPBEAT CONSIDERING THE RIGORS OF THE LIVES DEPICTED."
—WESTERN PEOPLE

ISBN 1-896300-11-1 PB $24.00 CDN • $19.00 US

FOR MORE INFORMATION CONTACT NEWEST PRESS
1-866-796-5473
WWW.NEWESTPRESS.COM